BIOLOGY IN ACTION SERIES
General Editor: DR. G. WATTS

THE FARMING OF FISH

THE FARMING OF FISH

by C. F. HICKLING, C.M.G., Sc.D.

LATELY FISHERIES ADVISER TO THE COLONIAL OFFICE

THE QUEEN'S AWARD
TO INDUSTRY 1966

PERGAMON PRESS

OXFORD · LONDON · EDINBURGH · NEW YORK
TORONTO · SYDNEY · PARIS · BRAUNSCHWEIG

Pergamon Press Ltd., Headington Hill Hall, Oxford
4 & 5 Fitzroy Square, London W.1.

Pergamon Press (Scotland) Ltd., 2 & 3 Teviot Place, Edinburgh 1

Pergamon Press Inc., 44–01 21st Street, Long Island City, New York 11101

Pergamon of Canada Ltd., 207 Queen's Quay West, Toronto 1

Pergamon Press (Aust.) Pty. Ltd., Rushcutters Bay,
Sydney, New South Wales

Pergamon Press S.A.R.L., 24 rue des Écoles, Paris 5^e

Vieweg & Sohn GmbH, Burgplatz 1, Braunschweig

Printed in Great Britain by A. Wheaton & Co., Exeter

08 103601 9 (flexicover)
08 203601 2 (hard cover)

Contents

Preface

THE farming of fish is a novel idea to many people, but in fact it is a well-established industry, though not, as yet, very widespread. In Britain the abundance of sea fish, and the disappearance of a public taste for freshwater fish (apart from trout), means that the traveller will see few fish farms. Because fish are creatures whose body temperature is the same as that of the water in which they live, fish farming is practised mostly in the warmer parts of the world where there is no severe winter to bring life in water, including the growth of fish, to a near standstill. But in northern China, and in eastern Europe and in Russia, cold countries remote from the great sea fisheries, natural production of fish is far short of demand; and there fish farming is being vigorously encouraged in spite of a comparatively low rate of production. Moreover, fish farming ties in well with the multiple-purpose storage or impoundment of water.

But fish farming is a practical application to food production, of limnology and freshwater biology; and that, in itself, is justification for a small book for those interested in natural history, and in the use of natural resources.

CHAPTER 1

Introduction

I HAVE been at sea many times on commercial trawlers and have seen a big catch of fish dragged up from the sea bottom and dumped on deck. Many times I have stood on the bank of a fishpond and have seen a big catch of fish netted in the pond and brought to the bank. But there was a big difference between these two lots of fish, a difference of ownership. The fish caught by the trawler became the property of the skipper and trawler owner only when they were dumped on the deck of his vessel. Before that, the fish had ranged freely about the sea belonging to nobody and everybody, and it was to nobody's interest to look after them so that more profitable catches could be got. But in the case of the pondfish, these had been the private property of the fish farmer all through; it paid him to protect them until they had grown to the most profitable size, to see to their breeding and the care of the young, and to their food supply; and to adjust the numbers of fish to the numbers his ponds could profitably support.

No one has yet been able to introduce the idea of property into the world's wild fisheries. All fishing countries are in competition for these fish, and all are sovereign states not subject to any law but their own. It is the usual experience that a fishery depreciates, in that it is always tending to give less fish at increased effort and cost. The reasons for this are now fairly well understood and so are the remedies. Partial success has followed many decades of effort to get some international agreement on regulations intended to protect the fish

1

while they grow; yet still the decline in the fisheries has not been halted. The only really decisive remedy, a reduction in the intensity of fishing by having fewer and less powerful ships at work, has always been impossible in peacetime. But in war-time it happens at once; and after each of the world wars there was a huge increase of catches and a complete recovery of the depleted fisheries. The lesson is obvious, yet its application offers great difficulties. As one of the British team of sea fishery research workers between the two world wars, I saw how advice on fishery management based on research failed against this international political background, and this is still the case (*The Times*, Nov. 10, 1966).

After World War II, I became Fisheries Adviser to the British Colonial Office, and saw big fish farms for the first time in Palestine (as it then was) in 1946. In 1947 I saw fish farming in Malaya, Borneo, Java, and Hong Kong. I saw that here was something different. Fish on a fish farm are private property. Therefore, though fish farming can never produce more than a small percentage of the world's requirements of fish, it holds possibilities of improvement in management and technique such as cannot at present be foreseen for the world's ownerless wild fisheries.

CHAPTER 2

A Historical Digression

ON LAND, mankind gradually changed from a hunter to a pasturalist. As a hunter, he had to follow the game he hunted; capture must often have been a violent and dangerous matter with the primitive weapons he had. As he had no control over the game, he could not be sure of success; days when he could gorge to repletion must have alternated with many days of starvation. Life must have been short and precarious, with few dull moments.

Then some people, somewhere, found that some of the uncertainty over the next meat meal might be avoided by rounding up and keeping in captivity suitable game for use as needed; and then they would have found that these captive game would breed and so maintain their numbers. So must have begun the association of man with sheep, cattle, goats, pigs and horses, perhaps because where this event happened these animals were the most easily domesticated. But *African Game Ranching*, in this series, shows that other kinds of game could have been domesticated just as easily.

A similar sequence must have happened with fish, the other chief source of meat for mankind. Fish were hunted with spears and arrows, were trapped in simple cages of various kinds, and were lured by baits to impale themselves on thorn "gorges" or primitive hooks made of bone or shell. These methods are still in use in many backward parts of the world. Later, when man learnt to spin threads, nets were used in which the fish either entangled themselves, or were surrounded

3

and dragged to the shore. The methods with nets which gave most fish were gradually improved and in recent decades adapted for the use of power, and in the open sea. At present they provide the bulk of the world's supplies of fish, a total of some 45 million tons annually. But the simpler devices are by no means dead, for modern forms of hook-and-line fishing provide most of the world's supplies of halibut and tuna.

These fishing methods, which are all a form of hunting, in fact the last and greatest of man's activities as a hunter, still have the hunter's uncertainty of success. He is still hunting wild creatures, whose comings and goings and concentrations and dispersals he cannot know with certainty at any time or place, and he cannot see them. All kinds of devices, such as echo-sounders and asdic, help to locate the fish; and a great mass of information and research is giving an increasingly complete picture of the life stories and movements of fish and the reasons for them. But still, a powerful modern trawler, costing perhaps half a million pounds, leaves port with no certainty what she will catch; she may return with a full load, or she may not catch enough fish to cover the cost of the voyage.

But primitive man had another kind of fishing—the battue or mass slaughter; and this also persists to this day in many parts of the world. Where there are alternate wet and dry seasons, the rivers and swamps may fall in the dry season until large areas of shallow water become isolated, with the fish in them. Then, usually on a date fixed by the local chief, who may be advised by soothsayers, these shallow-water lagoons are fished by hundreds or even thousands of people, trampling the mud until the fish are stupefied and can be caught by hand or by plunge baskets, hand nets, and spears. Fish poisons, harmless to man, may also be used to stupefy the fish and make them easy to catch. In this way, great quantities of fish may be got, enough for all, and to spare. An account of these fisheries may be seen in my *Tropical Inland Fisheries* (Longmans, Green, 1960).

Among the various kinds of water in which this kind of mass fishing can be done are river ox-bows. Rivers change their course over the years, and abandoned bends of the river may flow during high water in the rainy season, but become cut off from the main river when the water level falls. Such ox-bows are easily seen from the air in river valleys. Someone, almost certainly in China, must have noticed that the fish isolated in the ox-bows grew fast, and that if mass fishing were put off until towards the end of the dry season, a much greater weight of fish could be got than if fishing were to be done early in the dry season. From this may have come the idea that if such ox-bows could be permanently isolated from the river by artificial embankments and replenished with water through sluices, fish could be kept and fattened, and provide a larger and more reliable source of fish than wild fishing.

In China, fish culture in such ponds was already in use in 1100 B.C., so fish culture can claim an antiquity nearly as respectable as the culture of land animals. A book on the culture of the common carp, *Cyprinus carpio* L., was written in 460 B.C. This fish seems to have been chosen from among the wild fishes of the Chinese rivers as especially suitable for cultivation; and just as the first land animals domesticated, such as sheep and cattle, were propagated around the world, so the common carp has always been the mainstay of fish culture. But about the time of the Tang Dynasty, A.D. 618–904, the cultivation of four others of the local river fish began in China, in addition to the common carp, and these five fish are the basis of Chinese fish culture today. Now these species of fish are being cultivated on a large scale in Russia, and Chinese emigrants have spread their culture to the countries of South-east Asia.

In Europe, the common carp was brought from the East in the Middle Ages, and soon became the most important cultivated fish. Before that, there does not seem to have been much fish culture. From early settled days, moats and ponds belonging to monasteries, castles, and great houses were stocked, in the late autumn, with fish caught from the wild fisheries, and kept there alive for use as required during the winter. But this was more a matter of storage than cultivation.

Commercial fish farming for food in Europe is best developed in Poland, Germany, Hungary and Russia. More recently, in Europe and North America, the farming of trout has developed, in part as an adjunct to the sport fishing industry, to supply fish for stocking suitable trout waters.

In India, there has long been a simple form of fish culture, namely, the stocking of ponds, lakes, and irrigation dams with young fish caught in the rivers.

In Africa, probably because no settled civilization has ever been established south of the Sahara, fish culture is of very recent introduction. Simultaneously in the Congo and in Zambia (then Northern Rhodesia), the cultivation of the *Tilapia* fish was begun, in 1942–3. Fish culture has now been introduced to many territories in Africa, but has so far made but slow progress, for reasons discussed on pages 83 and 84.

The common carp, *Cyprinus carpio* L., which is probably the original cultivated fish, has caused problems where it has been transplanted, chiefly in America and South Africa; and this recalls the problems which can arise when domesticated cattle are introduced into countries already well-stocked with wild game. Though common carp have the advantage that their management is already well-known, whereas that of local suitable species is not, it is obviously better to cultivate local species if possible.

The African *Tilapia* themselves have become a problem where they have been transplanted to other countries. In the absence of natural checks, their very prolific breeding means that they will soon fill a pond with thousands of small and almost valueless fish all competing for a limited supply of food. This points to the desirability of farming those fish already native to the territory, and adapted to local conditions.

It is difficult to estimate how much fish is at present being produced in the world by fish farming. The great sea fisheries are mostly based on centralized markets where records are kept; but fish farms are scattered and may keep no records, so usually only guesses can be made.

In the State of Israel, however, the fish farming industry is organized into co-operatives which enable exact statistics to be kept, and these may be quoted as an example of how important the production of fish by fish farms can be. In 1963, there were 93 fish farms in Israel, with a total area of 4869 hectares, and these grew 9993 metric tons of fish at an average rate of 2053 kg per hectare, or 1891 lb per acre. But in most countries, as I have said above, only rough estimates can be made; and from them it seems that the total production of fish in fish farms over the world is about 600,000 tons. This compares with a total of about 45 million tons of fish produced by the wild fisheries. But a high proportion of these wild fish are not caught for human consumption but as raw material for fish meals and fertilisers. Probably fish farming at present accounts for about 4 per cent of the world's edible fish production. This is not a negligible amount, and it has an especial value because the fish can be marketed at times when there may be a scarcity of naturally-caught fish, since they are not subject to the fluctuations of glut and scarcity which so often afflict the natural wild fisheries. And fish farming still has great scope for expansion and technical improvement. What is farming? The *Shorter Oxford English Dictionary* is not helpful. "To be a farmer, to till the soil" is all the definition it gives of "to farm". But to me, farming suggests a benevolent interference with nature, whereby the land produces more of the materials needed by man, at the expense of the natural production much of which is not useful, or only remotely useful, to him. Thereby, also, the land is increased in value and productivity.

For example, certain kinds of plants, such as wheat, barley

maize, legumes, and grasses, which are valuable to mankind, and have been domesticated, are grown at the expense of other kinds, which are now called weeds and got rid of. Trees and bushes may have to go if they reduce production by shading, and the whole character of the soil may be changed by drainage, cultivation, and the use of lime and fertilizers. Where the produce of the farm includes animals, these animals are protected and encouraged to breed, while other animals which might compete with them or prey on them are killed or fenced off. A part of the fodder produced by the farm may be for the growth of these animals, and so the plant production of the farm will be in part converted into animal production, and sold as beef, mutton, pork, or poultry, milk and eggs.

Fish farming is very similar, though in this case the produce is wholly fish except in the Far East, for example, where the fishponds may also grow some edible crops such as water chestnut, water arrowroot, and water salad. A natural or artificial piece of water is cleared of water-weeds and reeds, and of fish, and is then restocked with desirable kinds of fish in the best numbers per acre. Useful plants are encouraged by the use of fertilizer, and fodders may be supplied to the fish to supplement the natural food supply. The effect of these measures may be seen in some figures of fish production in East Germany, a country with a short growing season and a very cold winter.

The natural freshwaters of East Germany have a rate of fish production of about 21 kg per hectare annually, and this is about the same as the freshwaters of Britain or America at the same latitude, or as the North Sea. But the fish farms had an average rate of production of 242 kg per hectare, or eleven times as great. So 14,000 hectares of fish ponds produced more fish than 151,000 hectares of wild waters. In terms of value, the superiority of the fishponds was even greater. For the produce of fish farms were all valuable fish, whereas the wild waters produced a high proportion of fish of little value.

The fish crop from the smaller acreage of fish farms was worth twice as much as that of the greater acreage of wild waters.

Here is a case where the natural cycle of life in water has been interfered with to the great benefit of mankind.

A fuller account of fish farming is in my *Fish Culture* (Faber & Faber, 1962), which is recommended for further reading.

CHAPTER 3

The Primary Source of the Material and Energy in a Fishpond

THE natural cycle of life in water is essentially the same as that on land, with which we are familiar. When the temperature rises and daylight lengthens in the spring, on land the grass and other vegetation begins to grow. It grows because the increasing warmth quickens the chemical processes within the cells, processes dormant at low temperatures; and because the warming of the soil allows the plant roots to take up water and its contained nutrient salts. The warmth and light re-start the process of photosynthesis which is the beginning of all new organic material. The new organic material produced by green plants is devoured by animals, such as sheep and cattle, which in turn build up material on which we feed as beef, mutton, or milk. As these mammals have a constant and high internal temperature, they would be able to grow and feed all the year round if food were available; and in fact at the time when there may be no production of new food material, such animals will be fed on stored crops such as hay.

In water, in spring, water plants begin to grow for the same reasons. These water plants may be rooted water-weeds, or they may be filamentous algae floating loose in the water or growing on stones, gravel, mud, or on other plants. And, finally, they may be phytoplankton, or plant plankton. Plankton means life which floats or drifts in mid-water, and the plants comprising it, mainly algae, are so small that, aided by various devices, they can remain suspended in the water. They are seldom large enough to be seen clearly with the naked eye, but may occur in such numbers that they may give a colour and opacity to the water. There is nothing on land which quite corresponds to this very productive world of small plants. They are disposed in three dimensions, and because of their small size they have a large surface area in relation to their volume, and as they are also transparent, they should be efficient at intercepting the energy of sunlight. In fact, however, other factors prevent anything but a partial use of the energy of sunlight.

The energy of sunlight is intercepted by the green pigments of plants, which are usually dissolved in special bodies called chloroplasts. Chlorophyll is really a group of pigments, of which four, two green and two yellow, are usually found together in the chloroplasts of higher plants.

The light energy intercepted by the chlorophyll is used in the reduction of dissolved carbon dioxide to carbohydrate, with the release of free oxygen, as in the formula below:

$$6\ CO_2 + 6\ H_2O \rightleftharpoons 6\ C_6H_{12}O_6 + 6\ O_2.$$

Because a part of the energy of the sunlight has been used to bring about this reduction of carbon dioxide, the carbohydrate formed (shown here as grape or fruit sugar) contains an equivalent amount of potential energy. For example, it can be burnt to give carbon dioxide and water, the reverse of the reaction above, and in burning will release the potential energy as heat. But, with the help of enzymes, which are organic catalysts, the carbohydrate can be made to give up its energy slowly, as needed, so that the plant cells can reduce nitrogen-, phosphorus-, and sulphur-containing compounds, and incorporate these essential elements in building more and more complex compounds, until the end product is protoplasm, or new living matter.

The whole elaborate but fundamental process has been summarized as follows:

1,300,000 calories of solar energy $+ 106 \; CO_2 + 90 \; H_2O + 16'NO_3 + 1'''PO_4 +$ traces of mineral elements $=$ 13,000 calories of potential energy, represented by 3258 g of protoplasm (106 C, 180 H, 46 O, 16 N, 1 P, 815 g of mineral ash) $+ 154 \; O_2 + 1,287,000$ calories dispersed in calorific energy.

It can now be seen how inefficient is this interception of the energy of sunlight by water plants. Only 1 per cent of the calories available are fixed as potential energy, yet this energy must drive the whole cycle of life in water. A high proportion of the light is reflected back from the surface of the water, and some of the light which does enter is lost by absorption on fine particles or in colouring matter in the water. But, as the formula above shows, most of the energy of the sunlight which enters the water is used up in warming the surface layer.

It might be thought that even a small increase in the efficiency of the capture of the energy of light would greatly increase the rate of photosynthesis, but this is not necessarily true. Photosynthesis also depends on other factors, and especially on the amount of CO_2. Photosynthesis will proceed only as fast as the variable in least supply will allow.

Using the new living material formed as the end product of photosynthesis, the water vegetation grows. The rooted waterweeds increase in size and put out new leaves and branches, the clumps of filamentous algae grow longer and denser, and the plant plankton cells divide until the water becomes turbid with their concentration. But the rising temperatures also call animal life into activity. Animals which may have remained dormant during the winter, or which may have survived the cold months as resistant eggs, emerge and find a well-spread feast of plant food around them. From there begins a chain or cycle of animals, with the larger feeding on the smaller, until, in a fishpond, we come to the fish which feed on the animals. And we feed on the fish.

In the Tropics, where there is no winter to break the sequence of events, the processes outlined above continue throughout the year, and result in a higher rate of production than where a winter slows or halts the turnover of material.

Once again, there is much inefficiency in the food chain. Between green plants, the primary producers, and fish, there may be four or five steps, though seldom more and often fewer. Roughly about 90 per cent of potential energy is lost between each step in the food chain. A fish, for example, which has fed on an insect which has fed on green plant material will get only about 1 per cent of the original material (calories), whereas a fish which has fed directly on green plant material gets about 10 per cent. This is one of the reasons why herbivorous fish are so important in fish farming: but unluckily there are few fish which are herbivorous and also acceptable as food for humans.

The loss of about 90 per cent of the calories at each step of the food chain is due to the energy consumed by the organisms in their life activities; and also to the conversion of some of the material into chitin and similar substances which may not always be usable by animals higher up the food chain. So far as the loss is due to consumption, the CO_2 produced returns in solution to the water to be re-cycled.

It may be of interest to note that land herbivores with warm blood, such as cattle, use an important part of the energy they obtain from their food to maintain their body temperature, and therefore have a transfer efficiency of energy less than that of water herbivores such as fish whose blood is about the same temperature as the water. Further, land animals have to use up energy in supporting their own weight, whereas the bodies of fish are supported by the water, though this is to some extent counterbalanced by the greater muscular effort needed to move through water as compared with air. Nevertheless, a piece of land used for fishponds, and growing herbivorous fish, can often produce a greater weight of protein than when used for grazing cattle. This superiority may be as great as 20:1 on poor sub-tropical soils.

So far, we have compared what happens on land with what happens in the water; but now we come to a difference which must be dealt with at length. The air is a continuous medium, a gas in which mixing is very rapid. It would be unusual, for example, to find big local differences in the oxygen and carbon dioxide content of the atmosphere. But freshwaters, at least, may be separated from each other and can differ a great deal in composition over short distances. Water is one of the world's best solvents for all kinds of materials, some of them dangerous to life in water. Finally, water is a liquid, and this greatly affects the mechanics of life in water as compared with life on land.

CHAPTER 4

The Water Supply

OBVIOUSLY, fish must have water in which to live, and fish farming, like other kinds of farming, can only be done where there is a reliable source of water. In places where rainfall is fairly evenly distributed throughout the year, fishponds may rely on direct rainfall. For example, a large group of fish farms in Hong Kong is run in this way, and so are some fish farms in France. Naturally, the level of water in such ponds fluctuates with the rainfall, but by filling the ponds rather deeper than necessary when heavy rains fall, there is something in hand for periods of scanty rainfall. But even so, during a long dry season the level of water in the ponds may fall very low, and then it may be necessary to pump water from ponds which have a little to spare to those which need it most. In this way it is possible to hold fish stocks over a dry season, though when the water is low fish may suffer from lack of oxygen, and may become especially prone to disease. However, the Hong Kong ponds have been run successfully for many decades, so that complete water failure must be rare.

Gravel-pits, sand-pits, and open-cast mining pools, which are often pressed into use as fishponds, may be kept supplied with water by seepage from surrounding land, and are, in fact, wells.

More usually, however, water to fill the ponds of a fish farm is taken from a stream or river, and the method is the same as taking water for irrigation. A dam may be put across a stream, so that its level is raised and controlled by a spillway;

then a canal is taken from the dam, leading along the contours of the land to discharge into the ponds. How elaborate these water-works are will depend on the scale of the fish farm and the amount of capital the farmer is ready to spend. Big farms will have well-planned concrete dams and cemented channels. At the other end of the scale, a ditch may be temporarily or permanently stuffed with clay to raise the water-level high enough to run water through a channel into ponds alongside the ditch.

Generally speaking, fishponds watered by the damming and diversion of a stream may be arranged in series or in parallel. When the ponds are in series, the water can run from one pond into the next, the feeder canal supplying the first pond. When the ponds are arranged in parallel, the feeder canal runs alongside the ponds discharging into each separately by a sluice as required. Each pond also empties independently into a drain, which is usually the old stream bed. The arrangement in parallel is much the best, because any pond can be emptied independently of the others; while in the serial arrangement water passes from one pond to the next, so that there is a danger of disease being transmitted with the water. But, again, it is a matter of what is feasible with the farmer's means. Usually, the serial arrangement is cheaper and this is the more usual arrangement with peasant scale fishponds.

Water may also be pumped to a fish farm from a lake or river, and with large fish farms this may be a cheaper arrangement than building a dam and water channel for gravity feed. In pumping, the water is raised to the head necessary to enable it to flow to all ponds along channels or pipes. The Malacca fish farming research station has a 36-horsepower electric pump (with another as a standby) which raises 1500 gallons a minute to a head tank, from which it can flow by gravity to any of the ponds. Now that small portable gasoline pumps are rapidly coming into use for small-scale irrigation, it can be expected that small fish farms will use the same kind of pump.

At Malacca, I sometimes used a 2-horsepower gasoline pump, easily carried about by hand, which cost about £40, and would pump about 100 gallons per minute, quite enough for a small group of fishponds. Water can be supplied to very small ponds by treadle pumps, or by Archimedean screw worked by hand or by a small motor.

CHAPTER 5

The Quality of the Water

THE water must be of the right quality. It must contain enough oxygen to support active life, and it must not contain harmful substances. Water that is poisonous to fish is infrequent in Nature, though water that has drained through pine forests or some kinds of swamp may have dissolved harmful substances.

In an industrialized country, rivers tend to be the dumping place for many industrial wastes. This is now controlled by strict rules: but at one time pollution of waters was so bad that a protest against it was written with a pen dipped into the polluted water, and was perfectly legible! Parliament once had to rise early, in Victoria's reign, because of the foul stench of the River Thames. Substances poisonous to fish, including cyanides and phenols, many of which are extremely poisonous to fish, may enter the rivers from gas-works, and paper-mills may discharge chlorine and lime. In the country, sheep-dips may bring poisonous compounds into streams.

More recently, the increasing use of synthetic insecticides and herbicides has brought a new danger. If washed by rain into rivers, or blown by the wind into water (as happens when sprayed by airplane or helicopter) they may cause massive deaths of fish, as they may be toxic to fish at concentrations of even a few parts per hundred million. They can even be used, under control, as a means of clearing a pond of unwanted fish (page 30).

Very poisonous substances can be secreted into water by

some species of flagellate, minute single-celled motile organ- isms, and these may cause great losses of fish. One flagellate, called *Prymnesium parvum,* in one bad year killed off a high proportion of all the farm stock of carp in Israel, and it remains liable to cause loss there. Fish themselves secrete substances into the water which become harmful to themselves and other species of fish when they become too concentrated. For example, in Denmark, where the small streams may have a succession of trout farms one above the other along their course, the lower farms may have worse results than the upper ones, because they have to use water that has already passed through many trout ponds. Similar experience has been had in Japan, Russia, Israel, and the U.S.A. It is quite distinct from a short- age of oxygen. That is why, in very intensive fish farming, there has to be a continuous flow of fresh water into the ponds, not only to keep up a good supply of oxygen for the fish to breathe but to sweep away the toxic by-products of the active life of the fish (page 47).

The commonest kind of deficiency in water is a lack of dissolved oxygen, usually caused by the decay (oxidation) of organic matter, either natural, as in swamps, or introduced, as in the wastes from milk and sugar factories, slaughterhouses, and sewage works. These substances may use up all the oxygen, and then the fish, and other living organisms which need oxygen, will die. Anaerobic organisms, that is, organisms such as some bacteria and fungi which can flourish without oxygen, may then take over and create the foul conditions which drove the Mother of Parliaments into recess.

In Table 1 is given the amount of oxygen, as milligrams per litre (which is also parts per million), which will dissolve in water from a wet atmosphere at a pressure of 760 mm of mercury.

The amount of oxygen which water can dissolve decreases as the temperature rises. Since fish are "cold-blooded" animals, which have the same body temperature as the water in which they live, they need more oxygen as the water temperature rises, for the rate of respiration may double for each 10° rise of temperature. So a rise of temperature increases the need of the fish for oxygen at the same time as less is available dissolved in the water.

The determination of dissolved oxygen in the water has until recently been done by a well-tried chemical method, that of Winkler. But recently an instrument called an oxygen probe has made it much easier and more rapid and convenient to get a simultaneous reading of the temperature and dissolved oxygen concentration in the water. The probe invented at

TABLE 1

Temperature °C	Dissolved oxygen mg/l	Temperature C°	Dissolved oxygen mg/l
0	14·16	20	8·84
5	12·37	25	8·11
10	10·92	30	7·53
15	9·76	35	7·04

the Freshwater Biological Association's Laboratory at Windermere, for example, is a simple electrolytic cell, with electrodes of silver and lead. A weak current passes between these electrodes, which can be measured by a microammeter, and the amount of current is directly proportional to the rate of oxidation of the lead electrode, and that is in direct relation to the amount of dissolved oxygen in the saturated solution of potassium carbonate which is the electrolyte. As the electrolyte is separated from the water whose content of dissolved oxygen is to be determined, by a membrane of polythene pervious to dissolved oxygen, the amount of electric current generated by the cell is in direct relation to the amount of dissolved oxygen in the water. Once the cell has been calibrated against the chemical method, it will give an instantaneous reading of dissolved oxygen and temperature, whence the percentage saturation can be determined.

When the dissolved oxygen content of water falls below a certain figure, fish will begin to die of suffocation; and the more active fish, and those which most need oxygen, will die first. Active predatory fish such as the trout and (in Africa) the Nile perch, die while the dissolved oxygen content is still sufficient for members of the carp family. Tench, especially, can stand low concentrations of oxygen, and is a useful farm fish for this reason. Mass mortalities of Nile perch are not rare in Africa, and are often associated with the flushing-out, by rainfall, of deoxygenated water from swamps or large beds of vegetation. It is plainly better to farm fish with a good tolerance of low oxygen conditions. Fish such as trout, which are valuable, are best kept in ponds in which there can be a constant renewal of water, though the rainbow trout (*Salmo gairdneri*) has a fair oxygen tolerance (down to $3 \cdot 0$ mg/litre) and can be kept with carp in stagnant ponds and even, formerly, in the sewage purification ponds at Munich. But the intensive commercial rearing of trout needs running water.

Spring water may contain little oxygen when it first emerges from the ground, and water from swamps may contain very little when it first emerges, because all the dissolved oxygen will have been used up in the oxidation of the abundant organic matter in a swamp. But when such poorly oxygenated waters flow for some distance in the air, and especially if they flow turbulently or over cascades, they soon take up oxygen from the air and can then support fish life.

The pond itself affects the water in it. Very small ponds such as ornamental ponds or ponds in which trout or carp are raised intensively, may have cement bottoms and sides; but this is too expensive for large commercial fishponds, which are excavated in natural soil. This soil must obviously be impermeable, that is, it must hold water without leaking. On sandy or gravelly soils, water may soak away through the pond sides and bottom, and gravel soils may act as "french drains". That is why fish farms are best built on alluvial soils or marshy soils. Sometimes ponds will leak at first, but should gradually become watertight as fine silt forms in the pond or is carried into it, and seals off the bottom. Animal dung, which is rich in silt, will help, and so will clay or marl spread over the bottom. Sometimes a pond may be made water-tight by mechanical means, such as rolling and impacting, or by trampling with a herd of cattle. Leaky ponds are uneconomic not only because fertilizers, both natural and added, are carried away or lost in the seepage, and the fertilized water then has to be replaced by new water, but because a lot of water is needed to replace the water lost. Where the fish depend largely for their growth on what the water itself produces, stagnant water is best, provided there is always enough dissolved oxygen.

Fish farms can be made in peaty soils, but the organic matter in the soil oxidizes, and not only gives an acid reaction to the water, but causes a shrinkage of the pond bottom until its level may come to lie below the sills of the sluices, so that the ponds can no longer be completely drained. It is a matter of history that the peaty soil of the Fens has shrunk, over the centuries, since the Fens were drained, until the level of the soil lies well below the tide-levels, so that drainage has to be done by pumping. Pond banks made in such soil may slump for the same reason, and because of this it is advisable to allow about one foot in four for shrinkage.

The presence of large amounts of organic matter in the soil, or growing on it, has an effect on the oxygen content of the water of newly-filled dams and reservoirs. The new man-made Volta and Kariba Lakes had, at least at the bottom, a low content of dissolved oxygen at first, because of the consumption of the oxygen by the decaying land vegetation now drowned. On a smaller scale, newly-made fishponds in the Congo showed a lack of dissolved oxygen when they were filled with water for the first time. One such pond, for example, which contained 8·7 mg/litre of dissolved oxygen at 23°C, or full saturation (see Table 1) when first filled, gradually lost its dissolved oxygen as the vegetation on the bottom decayed, until after 18 days there were only 1·02 mg/litre of dissolved oxygen. Not until after 40 days did the dissolved oxygen content rise again to 3 mg/litre, and thenceforward the dissolved oxygen rose to normal levels.

There is usually also a diurnal variation in the dissolved oxygen content of the water of a pond. This is to some extent

TABLE 2

Time of day	Temperature °C	Dissolved oxygen mg/litre	Percentage saturation
2 a.m.	29·3	9·783	129
6 a.m.	29·15	6·287	83
10 a.m.	29·1	6·675	88
2 p.m.	30·25	9·392	126
6 p.m.	29·6	16·342	215
10 p.m.	29·25	10·736	142

due to daily variations of temperature, for it is usually cooler at night and so, as Table 1 shows, more oxygen can be dissolved. But much more important is the reversible reaction shown on page 11. By day, in sunlight, oxygen is produced by the photolysis of water in the light reaction of photosynthesis, and the content of dissolved oxygen rises until, in the strong sunlight of the Tropics, the water may become very much supersaturated. This may be seen in a series of observations made in a fertile fishpond at Malacca, in the Federation of Malaysia, using the oxygen probe described above (Table 2).

During the hours of darkness, the process of photosynthesis stops, but oxygen is taken up by the respiration of plants and animals, and by the oxidation of organic matter, and carbon dioxide is released into the water. It should not be thought that respiration and decomposition at night cancel photosynthesis by day, for it has been shown that enough new material is formed in 1 hour's photosynthesis to last for many hours of respiration. In the example given above, the water was still 83 per cent saturated with oxygen even after respiration had been going on all night at the high temperature of 29°C.

In a poorly productive pond, there may still be some increase in dissolved oxygen during the day; but because there is not much green vegetation present and a great deal of organic

TABLE 3

Time of day	Temperature °C	Dissolved oxygen mg/litre	Percentage saturation
2 a.m.	28·2	0·641	8
6 a.m.	28·6	2·174	27
10 a.m.	27·0	2·199	28
2 p.m.	28·2	2·452	32
6 p.m.	28·6	1·957	26
10 p.m.	28·5	1·820	24

matter, the level of dissolved oxygen may remain low even during the day, and at night may fall so low as to reach suf-focation-point for most fish. This may be seen above in a series of observations made in an unfertilized and reed-grown control pond at Malacca (Table 3).

In this pond, swampy conditions prevailed, since it was a control pond intended to retain as far as possible the character of the original swamp from which the fishponds were made. Growths of reeds shaded the water, thus reducing photosynthesis and preventing wind action which might have brought more oxygen into the water.

The clearance of emergent vegetation, such as reed beds, is in fact an essential measure to secure fertile fishponds, and trees and bushes on the banks should not be allowed to shut off sunlight and hamper wind action. Muddy water, containing much suspended silt, can shut out sunlight, and so can the deep stains from some kinds of rotting vegetation, which can colour water brown or sometimes almost black.

In very still weather "blooms" may form. These are dense growths of plant plankton which develop into a layer at the surface which may be an inch or less thick. They may cause harmful or even dangerous dissolved oxygen conditions, for they shut out the light from the water below, and, while causing supersaturation with oxygen in the surface half-inch or so, may bring about an almost complete absence of dissolved oxygen in the water below this thin surface layer. This is a frequent source of fish deaths, and the remedy is to facilitate wind action and use mechanical means to keep the water mixed, and less generous fertilization.

Heavy rains introduce oxygen into the water, and so it can happen that heavy rain at night can raise the amount of dissolved oxygen when a fall could have been expected.

In fish farming it is important to see to the oxygen content of the water, not only because fish may be killed by suffocation, but because, even where there is enough dissolved oxygen to support life, a deficiency may reduce the activity of the fish, and cause unthrifty feeding and slower growth. And this will result in a fish crop below expectations, which is bad for business.

When fish are in distress through a shortage of oxygen, they will often swim at the surface with their snouts protruding, gulping air over their gills. When this is seen, the farmer must be prompt if he is to save his fish crop. Also, in this extremity fish are very vulnerable to birds, and this may often warn the farmer, who will go to see what is the matter if he sees flocks of birds hunting in his ponds.

He must let in fresh water, if he can, or use a pump to spray water from a fountain, or he can use mechanical means, such as beating the water with poles. It is surprising how much difference can be made by agitating the water in these conditions. But the farmer's best hope is for a breeze to rise, or for rain to fall; but, when the danger is over, he should find out why oxygen had become so dangerously short, and try to find a long-term remedy.

Swamp-dwelling fish have adapted themselves to conditions of very low oxygen content by developing devices for breathing atmospheric air. The nature of the device varies; but it often takes the form of a lung-like extension or enlargement of the gill chamber, into which project folds of tissue rich in blood vessels. The fish comes to the surface and swallows air and passes it into this lung-like chamber. Many of these swamp fish are valuable food fish, and some are grown in fish farms or are allowed to grow there if they find their way in. They include *Clarias* (catfish) species in both Asia and Africa, the gourami family, the so-called climbing perch *Anabas*, which is a small but firm-fleshed fish popular for currying, and the murrells, *Ophiocephalus* and *Channa*, of India and the Far East. These fish have the valuable selling point that, owing to their air-breathing organ, they can be kept alive for many hours in just enough water to keep them moist, in a hot tropical climate where fish preservation is difficult. The few fish found in the infertile pond mentioned on page 24 were air breathers, and so unaffected by the very low dissolved oxygen concentrations shown.

The swamps of South America also have many species of fish adapted to make use of atmospheric air, and some of these have become so specialized that they may drown if kept under water and prevented from coming to the surface to replenish their air-breathing organ.

It has already been stressed that wind action is beneficial in keeping ponds well oxygenated. Therefore fish farms should not be placed in narrow or deep valleys, which are apt to be rather windless; nor should there be bushes, trees, or reed beds which can ward off the wind and shade out the sunlight. But too much wind, especially in ponds of large area, can set up wave action which will sap and undermine the banks, leading to their collapse unless there is continuous repair work, which is expensive in manpower. There are various devices to give some protection to the pond banks. At least along the waterline, the banks may be revetted with stones or wooden slats. Or breakwaters may be made by planting lines of stakes in the water, or by floating rafts of bamboo which prevent the waves from breaking against the bank. Incidentally, break-waters are also shelters for young fish. Fortunately, in many countries the weather is predictable to the extent that the season and direction of strong winds are known; so cost can be saved by protecting chiefly those parts of the pond banks most likely to be exposed to damage.

The action of the wind is especially important in preventing stratification or layering of the water. Warm water is lighter than cold water, so on a hot day in a deep pond or lake, a layer of warm water may form at the surface above the colder water below (page 12) and there may be a sharp line of separation between the two. Exceptionally this can happen in very shallow ponds also. For example, at Malacca, which is in the Tropics only 130 miles north of the Equator, some stratification was noticed on a very hot and windless day in a large pond $\frac{1}{2}$ an acre in area, and only 3 feet deep. It was found that at two o'clock in the afternoon the water at the surface had a temperature of $32 \cdot 4°C$, while the temperature at the bottom was $31 \cdot 2°C$. But, at these temperatures, the specific gravity of the water at the surface would be $0 \cdot 9949$, while that at the bottom would be $0 \cdot 9953$. This is a notable difference, and the surface water was significantly lighter than the bottom water. It was also found that this lighter surface water contained 12 mg/litre of dissolved oxygen, which is a high degree of supersaturation, whereas the bottom water contained $5 \cdot 3$ mg/litre, or less than half, though in this case still about 70 per cent of saturation and ample to support fish life. The large amount of dissolved oxygen in the surface layer was, of course, due to active photosynthesis by the plant plankton, the lower amount at the bottom would be due to a lower rate of photosynthesis owing to the partial shading out of the plants by those nearer the surface, together with the greater consumption of oxygen by organic matter in the pond soil.

This case is quoted as a curiosity, for in such a shallow and very productive pond such stratification would be most exceptional, and also transient, for only a light breeze springing up and blowing over the large area of this pond would at once set up mixing of the water, the wind supplying the work needed to overcome the temporary equilibrium of lighter water over heavier water. At night, also, the surface water would cool to 28–9°C, and become as heavy as the bottom water, so leading to a complete mixing, with a uniform distribution of the dissolved oxygen at near saturation point.

In deeper ponds, and in bodies of water such as gravel-pits, mining pools, and natural or artificial lakes which are deep in relation to their area, stratification is commoner and may last longer, especially where the configuration of the land or the growth of surrounding trees prevents much stirring by the wind, and where the warm surface layer is too thick to cool down during one night to the point where stratification would break down. In such cases, the cooler bottom water could come, in time, to contain too little oxygen to support the life of fish or other creatures which depend on dissolved oxygen. Moreover, in deep stratified water, organic matter may continue to undergo partial oxidation in the absence of oxygen by fermentation processes catalysed by bacteria or yeasts. We are all familiar with one such fermentation process, namely, that which produces alcohol from sugar, with the evolution of carbon dioxide from the partially oxidized sugar:

$$C_6H_{12}O_6 = 2\ C_2H_5OH + 2\ CO_2.$$

This is only a partial oxidation, for the alcohol produced will burn, or explode in the cylinder of an engine, to complete its oxidation in the presence of oxygen and release the remainder of its potential energy. Though this familiar example of fermentation may not occur in natural waters, when the free dissolved oxygen has been used up, the products of other kinds of fermentation accumulate in the deeper water of stratified ponds. They come to represent an unsatisfied biochemical oxygen demand, an "oxygen debt" which must be paid off before the water can again contain dissolved oxygen. This debt can be paid off suddenly, as when there is an overturn and mixing of the water caused by a prolonged cold spell, or long heavy cold rainfall, or by a fresh wind blowing for many days, or by all of these. The "oxygen debt" may then be paid off from the oxygen dissolved in the former stratified surface layer, and the mixture may sometimes come to contain too little oxygen to support fish life. As the overturned water may also contain another product of fermentation, namely, sulphuretted hydrogen, which has an unmistakable stench and is also very poisonous, the mass deaths of fish which often follow overturns have been ascribed to H_2S poisoning: but the H_2S itself is a consequence of the lack of dissolved oxygen in the water.

Another well-known product of fermentation is methane, and it is often easy to collect a jar of methane by disturbing the mud at the bottom of a pond and collecting the bubbles of methane. There are bacteria which can obtain energy by oxidizing methane, thus making use of its potential energy, and these are at present under trial to see whether they can produce edible protein from natural gas (which is largely methane) and simple nitrogen compounds.

Because of the possibility of stratification, it seems that fishponds should not be more than about 5 feet deep for the best results. But, because fishponds built to these depths are expensive, some fish farmers save on capital costs by using ready-made ponds such as gravel- and sand-pits. Many such ponds are deep and would be rather unproductive; it would be impossible to drain them, they could neither be fished out, nor drained dry to expose the bottom mud to the sun and air (page 44).

The emptying of the pond is the best, indeed the only, way in which to take the whole crop of fish. Nets can be used, such as drag-nets; but unless the bottom of the pond is smooth and level, fish will escape under the net, taking advantage of irregularities in the ground; and they may also leap over the net. Fish poisons can be used, including some of the very toxic insecticides mentioned on page 18. The use of these might be dangerous, but derris is a natural fish toxin which will stupefy or kill fish without making them unfit for human consumption. Fish can also be stunned or killed by electricity, and there are many machines on the market for this purpose. But they are not so successful in fishponds as in streams, where there is shelter for the fish, for example under the banks. Fish will often remain in these natural refuges and thus come within the stunning action of the electric field: whereas in a fishpond, where there is no shelter, the fish move away from the noise and commotion of the fishing team.

Though the best depth for fishponds would seem to be not more than about 5 feet, the size or area will depend on how much capital, in cash or labour, the farmer is ready to spend. The larger the pond, the cheaper it is to make per unit of area. In temperate climates, where production per acre is low because of a short growing season, individual ponds may be very large, as large as 100 acres, and there are individual fish farms in Hungary of 2000 acres and more. Such farms are big business.

But in the Tropics, where the growth of fish is fast and the rate of production high, ponds tend to be smaller. On the peasant scale, where the farmer himself may have to build the ponds, individual ponds may be as small as 1/20th of an acre or less. But in such cases, the farmer may not depend for his living on his fish, but also have a vegetable and fruit garden, ducks, chickens, pigs, and sometimes mulberry trees and silkworms. One practical advantage of having fishponds as part of a mixed smallholding is that the farmer is obliged to visit his holding frequently for the sake of his garden and livestock, and is therefore likely to give some attention to his fish. Such mixed farming will be referred to again on page 84.

In Israel, where the climate is sub-tropical, with a long growing season, fish farming is an organized industry, with the average fish farm having an area of about 52 hectares, or 128 acres.

Tidal brackish water fishponds usually have a lower rate of fish production, even in the Tropics, than freshwater ponds, and so the individual ponds tend to be several acres in area. Where fish farms are on the commercial scale, the amount of capital which has to be spent is especially important, since interest on capital, and amortization, are usually the most expensive items in the cost of running fish farms.

As stated above, fish farms are rare in Britain, but in some parts of Europe they are a part of the rural scene, and are very attractive to look at: squares and rectangles of blue water among green fields, with well-grassed banks, and a red-roofed farmhouse surrounded by outbuildings and by fry and store ponds. Lines of trees mark the water-courses, one of which will have been dammed to divert water to the farm and its ponds, and bird life is usually plentiful.

In a semi-arid Mediterranean climate such as Israel's, the deep blue of the ponds is strikingly eye-catching in summer, amid the burnt browns of the land. In the Tropics, I think of a small fish farm in Borneo, run by a Chinese. A spring rises at the head of a shallow valley among a clump of bushes. The water flows through some marshy ground into a small pond formed by putting up an embankment across the valley, here still narrow. Further down the valley, a second, and much longer embankment, with a transverse embankment, gives two more ponds of about $\frac{1}{4}$ of an acre each. On the slopes of the hill above the ponds is a pepper plantation, with the pepper vines growing, like hops, on regular lines of poles. On the opposite side of the valley is the farmhouse, built up on pillars into two stories, the lower open like a porch and containing the kitchen and stores. From here the farmer can oversee his property and receive visitors. A small plantation of rubber trees, many fruit trees, and a vegetable garden are beside the farmhouse, and between the farmhouse and the ponds are fowl and duck houses, and hogpens where cross-bred pigs are intensively raised. Their manure goes into a cement tank for use in the fishponds and in the gardens. A ditch runs along the contour below the farmhouse, to lead heavy rainwater away down the valley and so to protect the ponds and gardens. An attractive and productive small-holding for a busy and contented man.

CHAPTER 6

The Basis of Fish Farming

FISH are the end product of a chain (or cycle) of events which begins with the process of photosynthesis by green plants in the presence of sunlight. Through photosynthesis, the amount of living matter is increased, and potential energy is stored up to power the cycle which leads to fish, and to us as eaters of fish.

Living matter is a very complex substance, but the essential elements which compose it are:

C, H, O, N, P, S, Ca, Mg, K, Fe.

In addition to this list of essential elements, there is a long list of so-called trace elements which are needed in very small quantities. The functions of most of these are unknown, but the need for them is shown by the poor or abnormal growth of plants and animals where they are wanting. These elements include:

B, Mn, Cu, Zn, Co, Mo, V, Si, and many others.

Manganese and silica are necessary for the growth of diatoms, and cobalt is a constituent of cobalamine, or vitamin B_{12}. Cobalt and molybdenum are associated with nitrogen metabolism in plants, and especially in the fixation of elemental nitrogen from the air. Vanadium can substitute for molybdenum in this respect.

Of the list of essential elements, the hydrogen and oxygen are mostly derived from water, and the carbon is got from the

33

reduction of dissolved carbon dioxide. The phosphorus, sulphur, and essential metals are all derived from mineral salts in the pond soil or in the inflowing water.

The nitrogen is derived from several sources. Important amounts may be brought down in rainfall, as ammonium compounds or nitrates from the upper air, where some is fixed by lightning flashes; and some is derived from forest fires. Probably most is derived from the relatively small quantities of combined nitrogen present in the pond soil and water, largely as nitrates and ammonium nitrogen. The great reservoir of elemental nitrogen in the atmosphere, where it forms 80 per cent by volume, is not usable by most plants. But a large number of plants are now known to have the faculty of fixing elemental nitrogen from the air, and incorporating it into organic combination. It has been estimated that this biologically-fixed nitrogen may contribute 100 million tons annually to the world's needs of nitrogen, and that this is as much as all other sources combined (including the application of artificial fertilizers). Most is fixed by higher plants in symbiosis with nitrogen-fixing bacteria (in Leguminosae) or nitrogen-fixing actinomycetes (in certain shrubs and trees). We should all have seen the nodules on the roots of peas, clover, etc., in which the nitrogen-fixers develop.

But many free-living organisms, bacteria and blue–green algae, also have enzyme systems by which they can fix atmospheric nitrogen. Blue–green algae contribute very large amounts of newly-fixed nitrogen in rice fields, and have probably enabled the same fields to produce crops of rice century after century. They are certainly a major source of fixed nitrogen in ponds, also.

Fixation takes place chiefly in sunlight, so these blue–green algae can fix nitrogen and carbon from the air at the same time. Organic matter and traces of iron, molybdenum, cobalt and also phosphate are needed, and the algae not only grow themselves at the expense of this new material, but secrete an excess into the water, at first as ammonia. This is taken up by other plants, and so enters the food cycle; while the blue–green algae themselves are eaten by animals such as the Cladocera (Fig. 3) and so contribute directly to the food chain.

The nitrogen-fixing blue–green algae are all filamentous. They can be recognized by the presence of *heterocysts* which are empty-looking cells with thickened cell-walls and often enlarged (Fig. 2). In the water of flooded rice fields in India, blue–green algae may contribute by fixation from the air as much as 80 lb/acre of nitrogen, equivalent to a dressing of 960 lb/acre of sulphate of ammonia, and without cost. In a lake in Pennsylvania, about 60 kg/ha of nitrogen was fixed by blue–green algae during the summer months from June to September, and this is equivalent to a dressing of about 720 kg/ha of sulphate of ammonia. Bacteria seem to be less important nitrogen-fixers in water than blue–green algae. For example, in a small lake in Russia, nitrogen fixation for the whole short summer period was estimated at $5 \cdot 0$ kg/ha by blue–green algae, and only $0 \cdot 05$ g/ha by the nitrogen-fixing bacteria. A fuller account of this process can be found in a very recent review by W. D. P. Stewart, *Nitrogen Fixation in Plants* (University of London, The Athlone Press, 1966).

From these and many other sources the plants derive the elements essential for the synthesis of new living matter, as summarised on page 12. It is the interest of the fish farmer to convert as much as possible of this new matter into fish. The difference between fish farming and the natural cycle of life in water is that, in fish farming, man can artificially increase the ingredients of the input, which are, light, heat, carbon dioxide, and nutrient salts, to get a rate of production much higher than in nature.

It would of course also be possible, and much more economical in material, to use the newly-formed plant material directly as food for man. Water crops used directly in this way include water cress in Europe, and water chestnut, water arrowroot, and water salad in the East. It is possible to use plant plankton as human food, and more may be heard of this in the future. On the experimental scale, as much as $14 \cdot 6$ lb dry weight of the algae *Chlorella* was harvested from only 1200 gallons of nutrient solution in 16 days, a rate equivalent to 8–17 tons *dry* weight of alga per acre per year. This was done by supplying nutrient materials in the best concentration, CO_2 to the extent of 5 per cent, as compared with $0 \cdot 03$ per cent in nature, and good conditions of heat and artificial light. But, at present, we prefer to take newly-formed algal material in the form of fish which have fed upon it directly or indirectly, even though, as was shown on page 13, there is a great loss of material thereby.

If artificial light of the right colour and strength could be supplied economically on the full commercial scale, as it can be on the experimental scale, photosynthesis could go on day and night, with a potential great increase in the output of new organic matter. If artificial warmth could be used to keep the chemical reactions at their optimum, in regions where a winter cold season slows or halts them, again, there would be an increase in output. Finally, if the amount of carbon dioxide and mineral salts available to the plants could be increased, again there could be a massive increase of production. But all these factors are interdependent, and an actual improvement in the rate of production of a pond will depend on the factor present in least amount. It is of no use, for example, to increase the amount of CO_2 available for photosynthesis, unless there is enough light to give optimum plant growth. In the Antarctic Ocean, the amounts of nitrate and phosphate which accumulate in the surface waters are greater than can be assimilated by plants using the amount and strength of sunlight available in the Antarctic summer.

So far, an artificial increase in the amount of light for photosynthesis has not proved economic. Artificial light may indeed be used, but for a different purpose, namely to increase the number of hours during which fish can be induced to take artificial fodders.

The benefits of higher temperatures are being explored. The optimum temperature for so-called warm water fish farming seems to be about 22–30°C. The rainbow trout *Salmo gairdneri*, a so-called cold water fish, has an optimum feeding temperature of 16–18°C, but continues to feed at 24° and even 28°C for a short time. In India, fishponds reach a temperature of 35°C in summer, and the fish seem to come to no harm. But above these temperatures, living matter becomes increasingly harmed, and life processes slow down until living matter dies. This is generally true, even though a few organisms are able to live in hot springs at temperatures over 50°C.

But, up to the optimum temperature, the chemical processes involved in photosynthesis tend to obey van't Hoff's Law, by which the speed of reaction increases at a rate which doubles with each 10°C rise of temperature. This is one reason why the rate of fish production increases with decrease of latitude. In northern Europe and Siberia, for example, the rate of fish production in unfertilized fishponds is about 70–80 kg/ha annually, in southern Europe about 220–50 kg/ha, and at Malacca, in the Tropics, about 314 kg/ha.

The records of the great Bavarian fish farming research station at Wielenbach give a further illustration. The production of fish was recorded from three ponds (always the same three) over an unbroken period of 32 years, and also the average annual temperature of the water during the growing season. The production of fish, expressed as kg/ha/annum, was greater in those years when the water temperature was higher than when it was lower.

Mean water temperature, °C	13·5–14·0	14·0–14·5	14·5–15·0	15–15·0
Mean crop of fish, kg/ha	78·2	86·0	92·4	112·3

Artificial heat is becoming possible for fish farming, with the great increase in thermal electric power stations. Very large amounts of heat run to waste in the water used to cool the condensers, and this heat might be used to warm fishponds and so produce summer conditions of temperature the year round. The Russians, who have a very cold winter climate, and also a great expansion of thermal power stations, are interested in this possibility. In many of their power stations, the water from the condensers runs into a very large dam or reservoir, where it gives off its heat to the air and is then re-circulated. In the reservoir, therefore, there will be a heat gradient between the point of discharge of the hot water, and the point of recirculation of the cooled water. These reservoirs are being stocked with suitable fish to take advantage of the warmer conditions.

One successful method is to keep fish in cages in the warm water, and give them artificial feeding through the winter. Later in this book this technique will be mentioned again.

It seems that the problem of using waste heat from power stations is more of an engineering than a biological matter. The waste heat is carried in a big volume of water, usually passing along pipes at a considerable speed. How is this heat to be transferred to a large volume of still or very slowly-flowing water in fishponds? It is certain that if this heat is made available to fish farmers at low cost, it could be used to boost fish production profitably.

Carbon dioxide, as a by-product of industry, has long been experimented with as a possible means of increasing plant production. Many years ago, in Germany, carbon dioxide, as a waste product of industry, was led experimentally through pipes, and released among the plants in potato fields. A great increase in production resulted. But, to enrich water with carbon dioxide would only be effective during sunlight: in overcast weather or at night, the pumping in of additional CO_2 would lead to the suffocation of the fish. In recent years, the amount of CO_2 in the atmosphere has been increasing as a result of increasing industrialization.

But it is easy to increase artificially the quantity and availability of nutrient salts, and many of the natural and artificial fertilizers used in agriculture are also used in fish farming, excepting calcium cyanamide, which is very poisonous to fish. Later in this book, examples will be given of the great increase in fish crops that can be got by the use of fertilizers. The subject has a special interest at present, because artificial fodders for fish are becoming scarcer and more expensive to administer, whereas fertilizers are cheap in both respects.

There is still a great deal unknown about the fate of fertilizers put into fishponds (as indeed there also is about fertilizers put on fields), but so much progress has been made because the benefits are undoubted, even where the best dosage is disputed. Ponds situated among fertile fields will benefit from fertilizer leached out into the ponds or into the streams which supply the ponds.

Though the use of inorganic fertilizers is increasing in pond culture, organic fertilizers such as farmyard manure from cattle, poultry, and pigs, are still the most frequently used. This is because these manures are a by-product of intensive farming, and may be available without a cash payment. Animal manures used are not only in the small fish farms in the tropical East, but in the big industrial fish farms of East Germany and Poland. The best dose is about 5 tons per hectare, though up to 10 tons have been tried. Though such manures contain nutrient salts, they are also largely organic matter, so that they are liable to bring about oxygen depletion when spread in fishponds. To avoid this, the manure may be placed in heaps, and not spread over the pond bottom, so that the oxidation of the manure proceeds slowly, releasing carbon dioxide and nutrient salts to be taken up in photosynthesis. In the Tropics, the brilliance of the sunlight may very much supersaturate the water with oxygen by day (page

23), so that at night there still remains a safe amount of oxygen. Also, manuring may encourage the growth of filamentous algae, and dense beds of aquatic vegetation; and here the oxygen produced by day may remain entangled as bubbles, which dissolve during the night, and so maintain a safe oxygen level.

CHAPTER 7

The Pond Soil

A POND soil must be impermeable to water, that is, it must be waterlogged; for, if it were porous and contained air, it would not hold water. There is a high content of colloids in a fertile pond mud, which has been described as "the chemical laboratory of the pond", since complicated physical and chemical processes take place there. The mineral basis of the soil will depend on the nature of the rocks from which it was derived. For example, a pond in rich alluvial soil may be naturally very rich. An outstanding case of naturally rich pond conditions has been found in the volcanic regions of Java, where warm springs flow over young volcanic soil. The result is a nutrient solution, which, in fishponds, may give fish crops of several tons per hectare per annum, without supplementary feeding.

To some extent the content of nutrient salts can be measured by the electrical conductivity of the water. Pure water is a poor conductor of electricity, so that it has a low conductivity; while the presence of dissolved salts greatly increases conductivity. For example, some rivers in Brazil and Guyana may have conductivities as low as 30×10^6 megohms, while the Nile has one of 174×10^6. But where the water contains soda, for example, it may have a very high conductivity, even though the sodium carbonate may have no nutrient value for plants.

In a colloidal pond mud, nutrient ions are to a large extent adsorbed on the soil particles, that is, they are held attached to the colloidal soil particles, and especially to iron hydroxides and carbonates, by negative electrical charges. When the electrical charge becomes positive, the adsorbed ions are released into the water and can be used by plant life. This effect can be modified by two factors, namely, the amount of dissolved oxygen, and the hydrogen-ion concentration (pH).

So long as the iron compounds at the surface layer of the soil are in the ferric state, they are strongly adsorptive of positive ions such as ammonium, calcium, manganese, and of negative ions such as sulphates, phosphates, and silicates. Nitrates and nitrites are not adsorbed, and so their effect tends to be transient, though important while it lasts. In reducing conditions, these salts are reduced to elemental nitrogen by denitrifying bacteria.

But when oxygen is cut off from the surface layers of the pond soil, the ferric iron is reduced to the ferrous state, and then has no power to hold the adsorbed ions, which are released to the water, often in substantial quantities. If these diffuse up into the illuminated layer of the water, they can be taken up by the growing plants, and so enter the food cycle.

It has been shown that there is usually an alternation of abundant dissolved oxygen by day, and of less oxygen at night (page 23); so, in a shallow and fertile pond, there may be a daily release of small quantities of nutrients needed for a day's active photosynthesis.

As to the effect of pH; when the water has an alkaline reaction, ferric iron adsorbs ions less strongly than when it has an acid reaction. It has been shown, for example, that at a pH of 6, thus slightly acid, 60 per cent of the phosphate in a solution was retained in a state of adsorption on a membrane of ferric hydroxide. But when the pH was raised to $8 \cdot 6$, thus strongly alkaline, the adsorbed phosphate was easily washed out of the ferric hydroxide membrane. Thus one of the many advantages of creating an alkaline reaction in an acid pond is the easier release of the nutrient salts present in the soil, or which may have been added to it.

The access of dissolved oxygen, when it is present, into the pond soil is helped by the burrows of worms and midge larvae (Fig. 3). The latter may occur to the extent of thousands per square metre, and their burrows resemble the action of earthworms on land in this respect.

The oxidation of the pond mud can be seen with the naked eye. When a pond is newly-drained, the exposed surface-mud is a bright yellow–brown, due to ferric compounds. But if this surface layer is disturbed, as by men walking about picking up fish, it can be seen that this brown layer is thin, and that beneath it is a deep black or blue–black soil, due to ferrous compounds. But, even as one watches, the exposed black soil turns yellow and brown, as the newly-exposed layer of ferrous soil grows a skin of oxidized ferric iron. Because, in this black reduced layer of soil, sulphur is present as sulphide, such soil may have a strong smell of H_2S. But as the soil takes up oxygen, the sulphide soon oxidizes to sulphate, and the smell disappears.

This important process of adsorption may explain why fertilizers added to a pond may remain active for many years. German work has shown that, even three years after an application of phosphate fertilizer, more than half of the original fertilizer effect is still present. Probably because of adsorption, not much phosphate fertilizer is washed out of the pond at each draining. At Malacca, for example, less than 1 lb of phosphate fertilizer could be found in the 880,000 gallons of water when a 1-acre pond was drained, though 30 lb (as P_2O_5) had been put in. The rest remains adsorbed in the mud, and is available for the next crop. But, even so, it seems that most of the phosphate is never used, a fact also true of fertilizer used in agriculture. Probably it combines with lime in the soil to form insoluble calcium phosphate, or apatite.

The soil of a fertile pond accumulates a great deal of organic matter, quite apart from any which may be added as fertilizer. This organic matter comes from plant debris and dead plankton organisms, and the waste products of fish and other animals. The long-continued accumulation of this organic matter may not only tend to use up oxygen and even create an oxygen debt, but it may retain reserves of nutrients which could be released by a rapid oxidation. So a dry period, during which the pond is drained so that the mud is exposed to the sun and wind, is a well-known measure to restore fertility. The soil cracks open and allows atmospheric oxygen to penetrate deep into the soil. Much of the accumulated organic matter is oxidized, and the mineral nutrients released for use by the next crop. In temperate climates this dry period takes place conveniently in winter, when fish growth ceases in any case. The production ponds are drained, and the fish removed to wintering or stew ponds, where they are kept until the time of rising temperatures in the spring.

It has been found that such a dry period may result in an increase in the mineral nitrogen content of the soil of as much as 142 kg/ha, as compared with a loss of 18·5 kg/ha in ponds which were not given a dry period. It may even be advantageous to grow a land crop during a dry period (as, for example, in early summer), as this may not only give some income but may dry out the soil more thoroughly through the deep penetration of the roots. A dry period also kills off the resistant stages of the organisms causing fish diseases, if any have been present. It is a fortunate fact that the germs of fish diseases are not resistant to a long dry period. But fishponds are to grow fish, and a dry period is only worth while to the extent that it improves the fertility of the pond.

Ready-made ponds, such as sand-pits, gravel-pits, and opencast mining pools are often unsatisfactory because they cannot be drained dry. I have seen undrainable fishponds which have given good fish crops for many years; but others have had to be abandoned after a few years because of falling yields. In the

Congo it has been found that the fertility of peasant fishponds declines rapidly in the absence of a dry period. Where ponds cannot be dried out, an alternative but laborious remedy is to scrape out some of the accumulated mud. This may be necessary in any case from time to time to restore the original depth of the pond. Shovels mounted on long poles may be used to scrape up the mud, which is floated away on rafts, to be spread on to market gardens or among fruit trees. There the mud oxidizes and releases its nutrients for the benefit of the garden.

CHAPTER 8

The Biology of a Fishpond

IN A commercial fishpond the fish are grown chiefly for human consumption; but sometimes they are also grown for sport, as when anglers are allowed to fish, and are charged for the time spent or for the catches made. This practice is spreading, for it much increases the income from a well-stocked fishpond. The fish will have grown at the expense of food grown naturally in the pond, or on fodder supplied, or both. In the latter case, they grow at the expense of food materials grown outside the pond. Carnivorous fish must be fed largely on food of animal origin.

The most important carnivorous fish grown in fish farms are trout and eels. Rainbow trout, *Salmo gairdneri*, are well adapted to fish culture, and are grown either intensively by themselves, or as a part of an intensive mixed culture including carps. In the latter case, they contribute to the total fish crop by using the same food materials, largely larval insects, aerial insects, and tadpoles and frogs, as they eat in nature; but, in addition, they perform in fishponds the very valuable function of controlling unwanted breeding in carps, by devouring the fry. This both increases the total crop of trout, and prevents loss of production by overcrowding. In these conditions, rainbow trout will feed at temperatures up to 24°C, and can stand short-term rises up to 28°C. They will tolerate oxygen concentrations down to 3 parts per million. Rainbow trout were stocked successfully in the ponds of the Munich sewerage purification plant, and grew well on the great abundance of insect, and especially chironomid, larvae developed in the rich nutrient conditions.

But because trout when they are grown intensively do need rather a large quantity of dissolved oxygen, they are grown in small deep ponds where running water constantly replenishes the oxygen supply and carries away the waste products of the fish. The food may be slaughterhouse offal, or trash sea fish, or, nowadays, ready pelleted food. To prevent a waste of these expensive foods, members of the carp family may be stocked in trout ponds to scavenge and salvage rejected food materials. In Japan, silkworm pupae are used as trout food; they have a very high protein content and so are mixed with a proportion of vegetable material. In intensive trout rearing, very large crops are got in a small area, and with a consumption of about 1 litre per second of water for about 18 kg of fish. The technique is lavish in the use of expensive foods of animal origin, and in the consumption of flowing water of high quality; but it pays off on the high price which people will pay for trout.

Eels need less oxygen, and are able to supplement their fodder by taking midge larvae growing in the mud of their pond. As there is a great wastage of food in the case of eels also, members of the carp family are stocked; and, since a dense plankton may also develop, these fish include the valuable plankton-feeding silver carp.

The intensive farming of the carnivorous trout and eel depends largely on feeding animal protein to obtain animal protein, and, of course, there is a great loss of material in the process. For example, eels may need 13 parts of trash fish to give one part of eel. A nutritionist might argue that it would have been more economic to use the trash fish directly as human food. But this kind of fish farming is useful because it converts cheap protein material into expensive protein material. It allows of the production of a large weight of fish in a small area; but, in the case of trout, it does need a lot of pure water.

There are few trout farms in Britain, and no eel farms; but trout farming is very big business in Denmark. There the fish are fed on small fish caught by trawlers from the sea. Rainbow trout from Denmark are exported to Britain and all over Europe; I have eaten them in Germany and Italy. Similarly, eels are a great luxury in Japan, and in countries, such as Formosa, where Japanese tastes and customs prevail.

The farming of carnivorous fish depends on a cheap and reliable source of animal food, and this is often not easy to get. But in the farming of non-carnivorous fish, the ponds themselves grow most or even all the food needed for the profitable growth of the fish. Indeed, because the giving of extra fodder is becoming less economical, especially with rising labour costs, the present trend in non-carnivorous fish farming is to increase fish crops by the improved use of fertilizers. These stimulate the natural production of fish food in the ponds (pages 65 and 66).

A food chain, or food cycle, has to be thought of; for, just as all flesh is grass, so is all fish water vegetation and especially alga. The new plant material formed as a consequence of photosynthesis is passed down a chain of animals to fish. Though the process is more of a cycle than a chain, since, as we shall see, much of the material is recirculated with an accompanying build-up and break-down of potential energy, the cycle is broken at the point where fish are taken from the pond. The material and energy represented by the fish crop must be replaced from a new source: so the process is more of a chain, leading from link to link to the final product, fish, where it breaks off. In a natural piece of water where no fishing is taking place, it would be correct to speak of a cycle, since the end product, fish, ultimately perishes, and its flesh breaks down again to simple substances which re-enter the cycle for recirculation.

In a good water overlying fertile soil, all the metallic elements needed for plant growth are present, but the rate of growth of the plants will go on only so fast as the essential element present in least quantity will allow. In the extreme dilution in which these substances occur in natural waters, they are probably completely ionized. Within the limits set by the temperature and sunlight and the presence of carbon dioxide, the greater the concentration of nutrient salts in the right proportions, the more vigorous will be the growth of the plants.

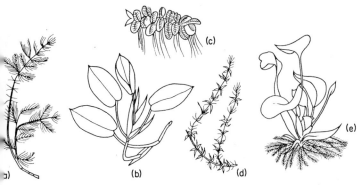

Fig. 1. (a) *Myriophyllum*, submerged water-weed. Stems 30–270 cm. (b) *Potamogeton*, submerged water-weed. Leaves 3–4 cm. (c) *Salvinia auriculata*, floating water-weed. Leaves ½–1 cm. (d) *Hydrilla*, submerged water-weed. Stems to 1 m. (e) *Eichhornia crassipes*, found chiefly as a floating water-weed, water hyacinth. About 12–25 cm high.

There are three main types of submerged green plants in ponds, able to use these inorganic salts and gases in the presence of sunlight. There are the rooted green phanerogams, such as the pondweed, *Potamogeton*, the water-milfoil, *Myriophyllum*, and the *Hydrilla* (Fig. 1). Then there are the filamentous algae, such as the pond slime, *Spirogyra*, and several other species of filamentous algae which grow attached to, and may come to cover with a thick felt, stones, firm mud, and other plants. Finally, there is the phytoplankton, a general name for the vast population of minute and mostly unicellular algae which float suspended in mid-water, and can multiply very rapidly (Fig. 2).

There are also some free-floating higher plants, such as the duckweeds *Lemna* and *Wolffia*, and the tiny fern *Azolla*. In the warmer waters of the world, floating plants may become serious pests. The water hyacinth, *Eichhornia*, which has beautiful flowers, is a world menace to rivers and lakes, by multiplying so as to impede the flow of the water and choke standing water; and the fern *Salvinia* is a pest in Ceylon and on the newly-

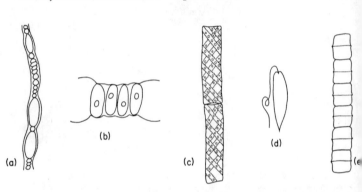

Fig. 2. (a) *Anabaena*, a blue–green alga. Cells 4–10 μ. (b) *Scenedesmus*, a green alga. Cells 16–40 μ. (c) *Spirogyra*, a filamentous alga. Cells 100–400 μ. (d) *Euglena*, a unicellular motile alga. Cells 40–65 μ. (e) *Melosira*, a diatom. Cells 60 μ. (*Note:* 1 μ = 1/1000 mm.)

formed Lake Kariba in Africa. These two plants are shown in Fig. 1. Yet in the Far East, the water hyacinth is cultivated in ponds as pig fodder.

The emergent "hard" plants, such as reeds and rushes, contribute little directly to the useful production of the pond; but many insect larvae, including Chironomid larvae, feed and take refuge in them, and herbivorous fish may feed on reed shoots while these are young and tender. Also, reeds may act as a substrate on which epiphytic algae and small animals may grow. But generally they are best removed. This can be done by harrowing out the rootstocks during a dry period, or by cutting them close to their base with the scythe or a mechanical cutter. At Malacca, I mounted a well-known make of (land) gasoline-driven grass-cutter on a raft of oil drums, and cut the reeds cheaply and quickly. Regeneration of the cut reeds takes place at the expense of reserve materials stored in the rootstock; but these materials are soon exhausted after two or three cuttings, and so the reeds disappear.

These green plants are the primary producers; but besides them are the blue–green algae, which are able, in sunlight, to fix atmospheric nitrogen as well as atmospheric carbon (page 67). They thus contribute both directly and indirectly to the food chain.

It has already been said (page 13) that about 90 per cent of the calories in the food are lost at each step in the food chain. Therefore the most economical fish to raise in fish farms would be herbivores, for they would contain in their bodies about 10 per cent of the plant material formed by photosynthesis; whereas a fish, say, which had fed on insects which had fed on plant material would have only about 1 per cent of the original material. We could, as has been said, collect the new plant material and eat it directly; provided we could collect it economically and prepare it in an appetising way. But in practice we prefer to take the material at second (or third or fourth) hand, in the form of fish which will have concentrated the plant material for us, and which are agreeable to eat, even though there is a great loss of material thereby.

The *Tilapia* fish of Africa are able to feed directly on plant plankton and on the filamentous algae, and two important species of *Tilapia* are direct plant feeders.(Fig. 4) The silver carp of China and Siberia (Fig. 4), and the *Distichodus* of Africa, also have fine filtration apparatus on their gills, and are thus able to strain off phytoplankton from the water. Some of the *Labeo* species of Asia and Africa feed on the felt of filamentous algae, which grows on the bottom of ponds and on stones and other suitable supports in the water. In the Great Lake of Cambodia the blue–green alga *Microcystis* is the dominant member of the plant plankton, and is the chief food of many species of fish, including the giant fish *Pangasius*. In the same lake, epiphytic algae, growing on submerged trees and bushes in the flooded forests, are food for no fewer than nineteen species of fish, including the *Pangasiodon gigas*, which grows to a length of over 6 feet and is probably the heaviest of all freshwater fish. Because of the high proportion of direct plant eaters in this lake, the crop of fish is the greatest of any freshwater fishery, and one of the most productive in the world.

The principal phytoplankton and epiphytic plant feeders at present cultivated are the *Tilapia* of Africa, some of which have been transplanted to Asia and America, the silver carp, *Hypophthalmichthys molitrix*, the catla (*Catla catla*) of India, and some of the Indian species of *Labeo*.

The aquatic higher plants are tougher, but several species of fish are adapted to devour them. Two of the *Tilapia* species have strong teeth on the pharyngeal bone, which grind plant material into small pieces, and these fish are farmed in Central and East Africa. The best-known, however, is probably the Chinese grass carp, or white amur, *Ctenopharyngodon idella* (Fig. 4), which eats not only the soft aquatic weeds, but also tough leaves of land plants such as grasses and the leaves of bushes, which come its way when the fish is living on flooded land in the wet season. In its pharynx it has teeth, operated by strong muscles, which are file-like or comb-like, and which rasp against a horny pad in the roof of the pharynx. These teeth rasp and tear up the plant material into small pieces, mostly less than 3 mm^2 in area, and so make the plant material suitable for digestion. Digestion is incomplete, and the fish passes out the material finely divided, but still containing about half of the original food value. This partially-digested plant material is a very good food for other fish, and in a fish farm the grass carp, which grows quickly to a large size, is always stocked with a group of fish able to use this waste material, as will be shown later.

Other plant feeders, though not so effective as grass carp, include another member of the carp family, the *Puntius gonionatus*, and members of the gourami family, which have already been mentioned as air-breathers.

Another extremely important group of very simple plants is the bacteria, because, though they are small or very small, they may occur in countless billions, and play an extremely important part in the life of water (and of life on land). In fact, without their activity, the cycle of life would slow down almost to a standstill. For it is bacteria which are mostly responsible for the breakdown and decay which brings nutrient materials locked up in dead organisms back into circulation. Without bacteria, life could go on only as fast as the replenishment of nutrients from natural inorganic sources, and this would be very slow, and therefore life very sparse.

Bacteria occur everywhere, in the water, in and on the bottom mud, and even on the walls of the plants and on plankton organisms, and on all surfaces. They are a very varied group, with great powers. Some need oxygen and cannot live without it; and some not only do not need oxygen but may be killed by exposure to it. As has been said, their most important function biologically is to break organic matter down to simple inorganic salts and gases, in doing so using for their own activities the last of the potential energy originally built into the new material formed in photosynthesis. They perform a large number of reactions which can be classed as fermentations, getting the energy they need not only by partially oxidizing carbohydrate, but by such strange reactions as reducing ammonia to nitrates and nitrites, sulphates to sulphides, carbonaceous matter to methane, nitrates and nitrites to elementary nitrogen, ferrous compounds to ferric compounds. What a vast number and complexity of reactions, many contradictory and all going on simultaneously, take place in the water and mud of a fish farm! But the net result is the breakdown of complex organic matter back to simple inorganic gases and salts, ready for photosynthesis into a fresh cycle of life.

Some fish feed on bacteria. In Lake Kivu in the Congo, the important fish *Tilapia nilotica* may feed on a large bacterium called *Spirillum* which is free-living in the lake water. The freshwater sprats of Lake Tanganyika may partly feed on bacteria. The many kinds of fish which are mud feeders, swallowing the mud, must get a part of their nourishment from the bacteria contained in it, as well as from the organic matter and animals living in the mud.

Some of the bacteria and fungi are parasitic, and cause disease and death in fish and other organisms. Even the tiny diatoms have even tinier fungi parasitic on them.

But returning to the green plants—the water-weeds are also food for many other animals beside fish. Water-snails, for instance, and many kinds of insect, find water-weeds to their liking, and these animals are good food for fish.

Many animals feed on the phytoplankton, and usually have some kind of filtration apparatus to catch and concentrate the material. The smaller animals are themselves planktonic, forming the zooplankton, such as the copepods and cladocera (Fig. 3). They have bristles on their feeding appendages which act as filters. Among the smallest members of the zooplankton are the rotifers (Fig. 3), which, with some of the smaller copepods, are especially important as food for young fish. The zooplankton are very important food-organisms for fish; for example, the cladocera sometimes swarm in such numbers that they give the water a pink tint. They are able to reproduce with great rapidity because they can produce a succession of parthenogenetic eggs, that is, eggs which develop even when they are not fertilized. Many fish feed on the zooplankton, for example, the char in Britain. Most of the important fish of Lake Victoria feed on zooplankton for at least a part of their life. A well-known farm fish which is adapted to feed on zooplankton is the big head, *Aristichthys nobilis*, which grows very fast and is excellent to eat.

There are also large numbers of animals which live on or in the pond bottom. Probably the most numerous are the midge larvae, the chironomid and chaoborid larvae (Fig. 3), which may occur to the extent of thousands per square metre. They

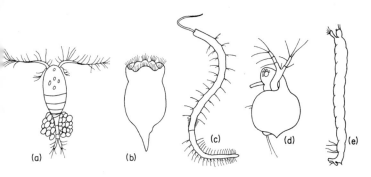

FIG. 3. (a) *Cyclops*, a copepod, 1–2 mm long. (b) *Notops*, a rotifer, 0·04–0·5 mm long. (c) *Stylaria*, an oligochaete worm, 5–18 mm long. (d) *Moina*, a cladoceran, about 1 mm long. (e) Larva of a chironomid midge, about 1 cm long.

may be so abundant that when the larvae metamorphose into adults, these emerge in flight from the water in clouds that look like thick smoke spiralling upward. So many emerge from the Nile at Khartoum that special lights are installed in the gardens to attract the midges away from the houses. One night I was in camp beside Lake Albert in Uganda, and we were having the evening meal inside a mosquito net. But each time the net was opened to bring in food, such a cloud of midges entered that we had to go outside to finish our meal, and so fell victims to the mosquitos. When the Zuider Zee in

Holland was dammed off from the sea, and the water remaining in the Yssel Lake was changing from brackish to fresh water, such enormous clouds of midges emerged from the water that motor traffic over the dykes was dangerous for some time. The nuisance was abated by facilitating the immigration from the sea of elvers, which feed on midge larvae; and, when the water became fresh enough, the ruffe, a freshwater fish (*Acerina cernua*), is now the chief predator on midge larvae and keeps them under control.

Midge larvae live in burrows in decaying vegetation and in the mud. Plant material placed in fishponds may increase fish production because midge larvae feed and grow in this material. In the pond soil, midge larvae feed on detritus, that is, on broken-down organic matter and dead plankton which has fallen to the bottom. Chironomid midge larvae are very good food for all kinds of bottom feeding fish. The common carp, *Cyprinus carpio* (Fig. 4), feeds on them as well as on zooplankton; and the soil of a newly-drained pond will be dimpled with marks made by carp nosing in the mud for midge larvae. In the sewage effluent fish farm at Munich, in Bavaria, the very rich feeding conditions nourish an excessive quantity of midge larvae, so the carp stocked in the ponds have a fast rate of growth, and give heavy crops of fish.

There are many other important bottom-living animals, such as worms (Fig. 3), which may feed, like earthworms, by passing mud rich in organic matter through their gut. Other tubificid worms live in burrows or tubes, and may have haemoglobin in their blood, to help them to cope with the low oxygen tensions liable to occur in the very rich muds in which they flourish. They are a very good fish food, and are often collected for sale to aquarists. In Hong Kong I saw a party of men collecting the long red tassels of *Tubifex* worms in a duckpond, the water of which was as thick and opaque as a pea soup with blue–green algae.

Molluscs too are important in ponds; the snails browse on

aquatic vegetation and especially on the algal felt which grows on stones, on the firm bottom mud, and on other plants. It has been found that, in Lake Victoria, they may excrete sulphuric acid, and so help to keep the essential element, sulphur, in circulation. The lamellibranch molluscs, such as pond mussels and clams, plough slowly over the mud, or lie half-buried in it, and feed by straining off the fine organic particles, including plankton, on their gills, which function as feeding as well as breathing organs.

Some of the water-snails are intermediate hosts for blood-worm diseases of other fish, and of men and cattle. Schistoso-miasis, or snail fever, is one of these, and is responsible for debility and weakness in waterside people where it is rife. As everyone must have access to water, the disease is wide-spread in the Tropics and sub-Tropics, and plays an important part in hindering progress. Because snails find their food on submerged vegetation, one means of controlling snails, and therefore snail fever, is to reduce this vegetation. This can be done mechanically, or by introducing ducks, or plant-eating fish (page 52).

Many kinds of fish feed on the bottom fauna, and among these the common carp and the mud carp, *Cirrhina molitorella*, are important farm fish. The grey mullets (Fig. 4), are very important farm fish (page 82), and some of them can live in freshwater, or seawater, or any mixture of these. Some bottom-living fish may have a protrusible mouth, that is, the jaws are so mounted that, when the mouth is open, the jaws swing out so as to form a downwardly-directed tube. This would clearly help to snatch out animals half-buried in the mud.

Because of their hard shells, only those fish can feed on freshwater snails and lamellibranchs which have special crushing mechanisms. The lungfish *Protopterus* in Africa, for example, is a "living fossil" which has flat crushing teeth, and includes molluscs in its food. Some smaller fish, such as the cichlid fish *Hemichromis* and *Astatereochromis*, feed on snails in Africa. In China and Siberia there is the black or snail carp, *Mylopharyngodon piceus*, which has strong crushing pharyngeal teeth. It is an important farm fish, and is stocked to feed on the snails which often develop freely in well-fertilized ponds. In fact, this fish grows so fast, and is so valuable, that it may get

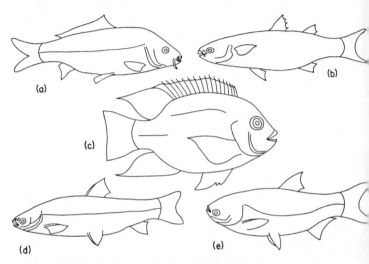

Fig. 4. (a) Common carp, *Cyprinus carpio*. (b) Grey mullet, *Liza* sp. (c) *Tilapia* sp. (d) Grass carp, *Citnopharyngodon idella*. (e) Silver carp. *Hypothalmichthys molitrix*.

supplementary feeding from wild snails and clams collected by the basket-full in ditches. These snail-feeding fish also help to control snail fever, and may be stocked for this purpose.

So far, we have considered only the food chain which begins with the creation of new plant material through the process of photosynthesis. But there is another important food chain which may be called the saprophytic food chain, from the Greek word meaning "decaying". This chain starts with the organic matter derived from dead organisms, animal and vegetable, and brings it back into circulation. I have said that the bacteria break down such material, but the bacteria themselves are food for infusoria, and for small animals such as rotifers (Fig. 3). Some lowly animals also seem able to use dissolved organic matter as food, and this dissolved organic matter may be very abundant. The infusoria and rotifers are fed on by copepods and cladocera (Fig. 3), and all these are good food for fish. This saprophytic food chain can support abundant fish life. For example, in Tripur State in north-east India, though the water and soil are acid, cladocera flourish in very large numbers without the presence of a photosynthetic food chain, and nourish an abundance of well-grown and valuable food fish.

So, in the ponds of a fish farm, a great many processes are going on at the same time. These processes, in countries which have a winter, slow down to near a standstill at low temperature, in accordance with van't Hoff's Law. But, on the whole, a pond must be in a state of balance with its environment, with some material being gained, and some being lost. Material is lost, for example, when marsh gas and nitrogen escape into the atmosphere, and when the adult stages of insects and frogs leave the water. But new material is always coming in, such as new nutrient salts with inflowing water, newly-fixed atmospheric nitrogen, dust blown in, and land insects blown in. Where fishing is taking place, material is also lost to the pond in the form of the fish crop, and this is what fish farms are for. To replace it is the fish farmer's business.

The rate of turnover of the gain and loss is determined by the rate of photosynthesis; which again is determined by the amount of sunlight, the amount of dissolved carbon dioxide, and the supply of nutrient salts. If the amount of oxygen released during photosynthesis is some guide to productivity, the example of the two ponds at Malacca (page 23) show by how much an overgrown infertile pond differs from a well-fertilized pond, when both are exposed to tropical sunlight.

This balance can also be regarded as an energy balance, and man uses that part of the energy originally fixed in photosynthesis (page 12) which remains in the fish at the end of the food chain, obviously only a very small fraction of the original energy. A great deal of the original potential energy remains as organic matter in the pond mud, and this is used by bacteria in their life processes, and returns into circulation either directly through the saprophytic food chain mentioned on page 59, or indirectly as the breakdown products of bacterial activity.

Tropical waters should be more productive than temperate waters for several reasons. Tropical water temperatures are high and there is no cold season, so organic matter will decay quickly, releasing carbon dioxide and nutrient salts for re-circulation. The high temperature and brilliant sunshine will give a high rate of photosynthesis. Animals in the food chain will grow rapidly, and the effect will be compounded with each link in the chain. It has already been shown (page 37), that, in the long series of observations made at Wielenbach, warmer years gave better fish crops than colder years. We could use the rate of production of fish as some indication of the quicker turnover of the biological processes in the warmer climates.

For example, fish crops from unfertilized and fertilized fishponds have been given as follows (Table 4):

TABLE 4

Area	Unfertilized	Fertilized
North Europe and Siberia	70–80 kg/ha	200–300 kg/ha
South Europe	220–250 kg/ha	600–700 kg/ha
Israel	90–100 kg/ha	300–400 kg/ha
Malacca	280 lb/acre	1500 lb/acre

The same can be seen in the produce of natural waters, subject to certain cautions. The most important of these is the amount of fishing being done, and the reliability of the statistics. A lake in which only a little fishing is being done, or where most of the area cannot be fished, will give only a low average fish crop per unit area even though the lake may in fact be very productive.

Below (Table 5) are given some examples of fish crops as kg/ha or as lb/acre (the two are nearly enough the same for the present comparison) in some natural waters.

TABLE 5

Water-body	Fish crop per unit area
Swiss and German alpine lakes	13 kg/ha
Freshwaters, Eastern Germany	21 kg/ha
Lake Mendota, Wisconsin	22 kg/ha
Lake George, Uganda	104 lb/acre
Lake Nakivali, Uganda	168 lb/acre
Lake Kitangiri, Uganda	282 lb/acre
Ponds fed by hot springs, Trogong, Java	2000–10,000 kg/ha

In European and North American waters, active growth for most fishes is restricted to only about 200 days in the year, and even so, at lower temperatures and a slower rate than in the tropics. So fish farming is more likely to be productive and profitable in warmer than in colder climates; and this is just as well, for the need for increased supplies of fish is greatest in the warmer tropical countries. Unluckily, lack of capital and other socio-economic factors may prevent full advantage being taken of these favourable conditions, as will be shown later.

CHAPTER 9

Fish Farming

IN FISH farming we can alter to our advantage a number of factors in the natural cycle of life in ponds. We can remove unwanted vegetation, and unwanted species of fish which might compete with, or prey upon, the more valuable species of fish it is desired to cultivate. Each pound of predatory fish may have to be paid for with the loss of many pounds of non-predatory fish.

The best way in which to get rid of unwanted fish is to drain the pond dry by opening the sluices, and remove all the fish; or, where the pond cannot be drained dry, to use a suitable fish poison to kill off all the fish. The ponds can then be restocked with desirable and valuable fish in the right numbers per hectare or per acre. Too many fish would mean that the food available for them would be shared among too many individual fish, with only a little for each. As the fish are also using up the energy from their food to maintain their life processes, overstocking of the pond will result in there being no surplus food over and above maintenance requirements to give any growth. There would be zero fish production. On the other hand, too few fish stocked would lead to an incomplete use of the food available, and so, again, to a rate of production below the best. So the rate of stocking of fish to give the best results is quite a complicated matter, and will be discussed more fully later. Obviously, it has a most important effect on the size of the fish crop. It is analogous to the spacing of a land crop, and to the removal of competing weeds.

It was said on page 39 that the amount and composition of the nutrient salts is the easiest of the factors to change, which might increase the rate of photosynthesis, and so the rate of synthesis of new plant material. For example, the addition of phosphate fertilizer to fishponds in Germany increased the fish crop by 80 per cent, and was very profitable, since the value of the extra weight of fish got was 8 to 10 times the cost of the fertilizer and the cost of spreading it.

Because of the rising costs of labour, and the increasing difficulty of obtaining suitable cheap fodders for fish, the present trend in fish farming is to get the largest possible crops from the use of fertilizers alone, and much study is being put into this in many countries. Examples will be given later.

An essential preliminary to the addition of fertilizer is the addition of lime where the water has not already a natural high lime content and an alkaline reaction. In any case, calcium is one of the essential elements. Slaked lime is also used to clear ponds of fish diseases and parasites, and as a fish poison, since the very alkaline and caustic reaction which results when slaked lime is spread in water is an effective poison.

But the chief use for lime in fish farming is to ensure an alkaline reaction, and a reserve of base in the water, where this is not naturally present. Tables are available to indicate how much lime is needed at various levels of soil and water acidity, and this also varies with the nature of the soil, for larger quantities are needed on clay than on sandy soils.

Obviously, the cheapest source of lime will be used, and this must take transport costs into account. Where transport costs are high, it would be cheaper to buy quicklime, since it weighs only half as much as limestone for the same CaO content. One of the advantages of basic slag as a fertilizer is its high content of lime as well as its phosphate content. So it is useful to use in acid conditions.

At Malacca I used limestone powder, the waste limestone which falls through the screens when limestone is being graded.

As it is a by-product, it is cheap; and as I bought by the lorry-load, the combined cost of limestone and delivery to site was reasonable.

But we had to deal with water of extreme acidity on many occasions, due to sulphuric acid derived from the oxidation of sulphides in the soil. At a pH of less than about 4, due to this dilute sulphuric acid, calcium carbonate becomes ineffective as a neutralizing agent, because of the calcium sulphate (gypsum) produced is only slowly soluble in water. A sludge of slaked lime may have to be used in very acid conditions.

Acid water is less productive than alkaline or neutral water for many reasons. It may affect adversely the life-processes of fish and other organisms; for example, fish may cease to feed. Fish are more vulnerable to diseases and parasites in acid water. Very acid water will kill fish.

An alkaline reaction in the water promotes the breakdown of organic matter, and the release of the nutrient salts; it also releases nutrient ions from adsorption (page 42). An alkaline reaction tends to flocculate colloidal organic matter. But most importantly, an excess of base, often occurring as soda in Nature, but also in Nature, and always in fish farming, as lime, has a buffering effect, preventing wide fluctuations in acidity: and can hold large reserves of CO_2 in solution as bicarbonates. This is expressed in the reversible reaction:

$$CaCO_3 + H_2O + CO_2 \rightleftarrows Ca(HCO_3)_2$$

Lime is dissolved by carbonic acid to go into solution as calcium bicarbonate, and thereby the water is prevented from being made acid by carbonic acid. The presence of lime therefore buffers the water, damping down changes in pH.

Conversely, when green plants are using up the CO_2 dissolved in the water for their photosynthesis, the above reaction goes into reverse. The bicarbonate dissociates into CO_2, water, and limestone. The CO_2 is taken up for photosynthesis, and the insoluble limestone is deposited as a fine white powder. I remember seeing a fishpond in Jamaica, where the soil is very calcareous, in the bright sunshine of early afternoon. The water-weeds, stones, etc., in the pond were well-dusted with fine white chalk deposited from the water. At night, when photosynthesis stops and the respiration of plants and animals produces carbon dioxide, the deposited chalk goes into solution again as calcium bicarbonate. By thus holding a reserve of carbon dioxide in solution in the form of easily-dissociated bicarbonates, the presence of lime makes it unlikely that a lack

TABLE 6

Treatment of the ponds	Fish crop, lb/acre/6 months	
	Range	Average
6 ponds with limestone only	71–136	93
6 ponds with 20 lb/acre P_2O_5 only	165–296	217
6 ponds with 20 lb/acre P_2O_5 and limestone	205–486	344
6 ponds with 15 lb/acre K_2O and limestone	50–186	102
6 ponds with 20 lb P_2O_5 and 15 lb/acre K_2O and limestone	116–379	267

of CO_2 would be the limiting factor in the production of new plant material, and thence down the chain to fish.

One of the trials done at Malacca (Table 6) may serve to illustrate the effect of lime on fish production.

The six ponds fertilized with superphosphate alone gave a much smaller crop of fish than the six treated with superphosphate and limestone, and show the advantage of supplying lime to ponds where it is naturally in short supply.

The table also shows that the addition of potash, either alone or with phosphate, did not give a better fish crop than phosphate alone; and it is the general experience that potash is seldom a limiting element in plant nutrition, except in ponds made in peaty soil, which are often short of this element.

Except in such cases, the use of potash fertilizer seems to have been generally abandoned.

The need for fertilizers containing nitrogen has not been settled satisfactorily. On the land, they are very important in increasing crops of all kinds, but in fishponds their effect is often uncertain. The classical German researches on this matter before and immediately after the First World War showed that the fish crops got were just as good without added nitrogen fertilizer as with it, whence the German practice of

TABLE 7

Treatment of the ponds	Fish crop, lb/acre/6 months	
	Range	Average
(a) 6 ponds with limestone only	66–225	140
(b) 6 ponds with limestone + 40 lb/acre P_2O_5	340–980	703
(c) 6 ponds with limestone + 60 lb/acre P_2O_5	575–1012	742
(d) 6 ponds with limestone + 40 lb/acre P_2O_5 + 25 lb/acre N as urea	504–766	662
(e) 6 ponds with limestone + 40 lb/acre P_2O_5 + 25 lb/acre N as urea + 15 lb/acre K_2O	435–759	598
(f) 6 ponds with limestone + 40 lb/acre P_2O_5 + 25 lb/acre $Ca(NO_3)_2$ + 15 lb/acre K_2O N as urea	505–950	654

nitrogenless fertilization. Why spend money on a nitrogen fertilizer if as good a crop of fish can be got without it?

Trials made at Malacca give results similar to those got by the German workers, as may be seen in Table 7.

All the fertilizer treatments gave far better results than treatment with limestone only. The best result (treatment c) was with limestone and 60 lb/acre of P_2O_5, given as triple superphosphate. A dose of 40 lb/acre of P_2O_5 (treatment b) gave nearly as good a fish crop as 60 lb, showing that in this case the extra 20 lb/acre of P_2O_5 did not give a proportionate increase in the fish crop.

Treatments d, e, and f, in which nitrogen fertilizer was given to the extent of 25 lb/acre N, gave no better results than phosphate fertilizer alone (treatments b and c), whether the nitrogen was given as urea alone, or with potash, or as calcium nitrate (air saltpetre) with potash.

This puzzling but very useful finding means that the protein of fish flesh, which contains an important quantity of combined nitrogen, can be grown in a fishpond from sources of nitrogen developed in the pond itself. At Malacca, for example, some ponds have given four or five crops of fish in succession, totalling in all between a ton, and a ton and a half. The quantity of nitrogen contained in this weight of fish crop is far greater than that contained in the pond water, which is naturally poor in nitrogen compounds. It seems certain that we have to thank the blue–green algae for this free replenishment of combined nitrogen, fixed from the nitrogen of the atmosphere (page 35). This would explain the uncertainty of the results of giving nitrogenous fertilizer. For if the blue–green algae are given combined nitrogen as fertilizer, they behave like other plants, and use this combined nitrogen for their growth. But if they are grown in the absence of sufficient combined nitrogen, they will fix their own supply from the atmospheric elemental nitrogen, often in large quantities, and even secrete a surplus into the water for other plants to use.

Using the best combinations of fertilizer, and stocking the ponds with the optimum number of fish, some very high rates of production can be achieved. Even in the Moscow region, where the growing season is short, rates of fish production as high as 800 kg/ha have been got. The cost of fertilizers was less than one-third of the cost of fodders which would have been given to get the same increase of weight. At Malacca, fish crops as high as 2500 lb/acre have been got with fertilizer alone. Phosphorus is clearly the key element in pond fertilization; but lately there has been evidence that, at least in temperate climates, the ratio of phosphorus to nitrogen may be limiting.

It is not always possible to see the effect of the added fertilizer. Sometimes there is an obvious outburst of plant growth
following fertilization, so much so that there may be an un-
consumed surplus in the pond at harvest. But if the pond is
stocked with plant-eating fish, or if the pond already has a good
population of zooplankton, the increased plant population will
at once be grazed down as fast as it is developed, and then the
greatly increased fish crop may be the only visible result of
applying fertilizers. When the ponds have been harvested, the
unfertilized control pond bottoms look very barren and bare
as compared with the fertilized ponds, which always have
vegetation and other manifestations of abundant life.

The so-called artificial or chemical fertilizers have only been
in use for the last eighty years or so, and then only among some
of the fish farmers in the more advanced countries. Where fish
farming is on the peasant level, these fertilizers are little used
as yet, but organic fertilizers such as dung, which are by-
products of other forms of farming, and of which the nutrient
materials are thus brought back into circulation.

It has for long been regarded as a paradox, that we allow
vast quantities of plant nutrients to go to waste in sewage, while
at the same time farmers must spend large sums of money on
buying fertilizers to maintain or increase plant production.
Not all this is wholly lost, however, for the plant nutrients contained in London's sewage, discharged into the southern North
Sea, support a rich growth of plankton, which can be traced
well into the middle of the Southern Bight. This enrichment of
the sea in turn supports about a half of all the commercially
important fish caught in the southern North Sea.

But modern sewage treatment not only salvages valuable
solid fertilizers, but produces a clarified effluent rich in organic
matter and nutrient salts. When this effluent is suitably diluted
and passed through fishponds, it is a very rich fertilizer, and
gives very large crops of fish, which feed on the vast numbers of
midge larvae (Fig. 3) and crustacea resulting from the plant

life produced by such fertilization. The Munich City sewage fishponds give carp crops up to 600 kg/ha, or better than crops got with heavy supplementary foddering. The Berlin sewage field-filtration effluent, when passed through fishponds, gave a natural growth of carp of 800–900 kg/ha. Finally, the treated sewage of the central Polish town of Kielce, introduced undiluted into carp ponds, gave the remarkable crop of 1300 kg/ha.

Raw sewage placed in ponds in central Europe may give fish crops up to 600 kg/ha, and in the tropical conditions of Java, raw sewage gave fish crops of 3000–4000 kg/ha per annum.

As treated sewage effluent, and still more, raw sewage, contains enough organic matter to use up all the dissolved oxygen in a pond, and so cause the death of the fish, precautions have to be taken. The effluent may be diluted 3 or 4 to 1 with water; or, as in India where cattle dung is much used, the organic matter may be placed in heaps so that oxidation is slow. But one safeguard is that, as shown on page 23, a richly fertilized pond may grow such abundant plant life that supersaturation with oxygen during the day keeps up a safe oxygen level through the night; a second safeguard is that filamentous algae and beds of vegetation may hold masses of bubbles of oxygen, which dissolve during the night and keep up the supply.

CHAPTER 10

The Stocking of Fishponds

I HAVE said that one reason for the high rate of production on fish farms is the removal of unwanted fish from the ponds which might compete with, or prey upon, the desirable fish. But which are the desirable fish, and how many should be stocked?

They must obviously be popular kinds of fish which will sell at a good price. They must also be fish which will grow fast on the foods growing in the pond, or which are added as fodder, and they must be hardy.

It is being recognized everywhere that great advantages result from the growing together in the same pond of two or more species of fish with different feeding habits. It has been shown that a pond produces a wide variety of foods, such as plants, algae, plankton, worms, insects; and others may be added as fodders. Though most fish are adaptable feeders, a more complete use of the natural produce of the pond is got by multi-species stocking. The analogy is with cattle and game, in the fine booklet in this series *African Game Ranching*. It is there shown that land can support a far greater population of game, and without harm to the soil, than of cattle: for the latter feed largely on the ground crops of grass, etc., whereas the game includes browsers on trees and bushes, thus making better use of the production of the land.

In Germany and other European countries, there is practically a monoculture of the common carp, *Cyprinus carpio* (Fig. 4), though the tench, *Tinca tinca*, may be grown as well in the same ponds. These two fish have similar feeding habits, but at least the farmer has two different kinds of fish to sell. In Israel, the fish farmers have for years been looking for fish of different habits to stock with the common carp in their fish farms. They have had good success with the *Tilapia* fish, which is a plankton and algal browser, and the grey mullet, which feeds on algal felts and detritus. I have seen figures showing that in Israel a mixed stocking with carp, *Tilapia*, and grey mullet may give a fish crop as high as 2500 kg/ha, where carp alone would give 1500 kg/ha.

This growing together in the same pond of fish of complementary feeding habits has been carried furthest in the Chinese system of traditional fish farming, which is now being adapted in other countries. In this system, the principal fish are:

Grass carp or White amur *Ctenopharyngodon idella*	Plant eater
Silver carp or White tolstolobik *Hypothalmichthys molitrix*	Phytoplankton eater
Big head or Variegated tolstolobik *Aristichthys nobilis*	Zooplankton feeder
Common carp *Cyprinus carpio*	Bottom feeder

In addition, in Hong Kong and Formosa, the grey mullet, *Mugil* sp., is stocked in large numbers with the above four fish.

In mainland China two more fish yet may be grown with some or all of the above. These are:

Black or Snail carp *Mylopharyngodon piceus*	Feeder on molluscs
Mud carp *Cirrhina molitorella*	Bottom feeder

In Indonesia, the giant gorami, *Osphronemus olfax*, and the tawes, *Puntius gonionatus*, both plant feeders, are grown with the kissing gorami, *Helostoma temmincki*, and the nilem, *Osteochilus hasselti*, both plankton and algal felt feeders, and the common carp.

It is hardly possible for one fish farm to have the means of breeding all these species; so there is an ancillary fish fry or fish seed industry, from which fish farmers can buy their requirements. For example, in Calcutta there is a big fish seed market where millions of fry are bought and sold daily in the season. Hong Kong has an important export trade, by sea and air, in the fry of the Chinese major carps. Recent improvements in fish-breeding techniques have made dealers largely independent of naturally spawned fry. All the major Indian and Chinese carps are now induced to spawn by the injection of hormones usually prepared from the pituitary glands of fish.

The fry are nowadays sent by air in polythene bags in water under an atmosphere of oxygen. The size of the individual fry will depend on the species and the demand of the customer. Obviously, very small and young fry will travel many more to the container than big fry, and so be cheaper. But more may die in transit, and the survivors will have to be nursed in fry ponds before stocking in the production ponds. On the other hand, large fingerlings of 2 to 3 inches (4–6 cm) will travel only a few dozen to the container, and so be expensive to buy and transport; but they will be past the dangers of infancy and can be stocked immediately in the production ponds. The fish farmer must judge for himself which is the better business.

The number of fish fry or fingerlings stocked must be carefully controlled. There may be considerable mortality among the fry stocked, especially if young fry are bought. A loss of 30 per cent of grass carp stocked is not uncommon in fishpond experience, and such losses must be allowed for when reckoning the numbers of fish to stock per acre or hectare. The surviving fish must be of the right number to be able to use up the food produced in or supplied to the pond, but not so many that they compete with each other and so reduce the amount available for the growth of each fish. The number will evidently also have to take into account the treatment of the pond. A well-fertilized pond will stand a heavier rate of stocking than an unfertilized pond.

We must think of a "maximum standing crop" of fish. This is the total weight of fish which a pond can support without gain or loss. It could consist of a smaller number of larger fish, or of a larger number of smaller fish; which the fish farmer would choose would depend on what size of fish earns the most money. Usually, larger fish sell for more money, per pound or per kilo, than smaller fish, and there is good reason for this preference. Small fish have relatively less edible meat than larger fish. I can illustrate this (Table 8) with the fish *Tilapia mossambica*.

TABLE 8

Weight of fish	Percentage of fish giving edible fillets
1·1 lb	24
1·5 lb	27
4·8 lb	46

A fish of, say, 2 lb weight will give more edible meat than four fish of ½ lb weight each, and will sell for more money.

The growth in total weight of a batch of newly-stocked fish follows an S-shaped curve, as shown in Fig. 5 for conditions where there is no seasonal check in growth.

The fish stocked will be small or very small, probably some hundreds or thousands of specimens, of a total weight of only a few pounds or kilograms. At first, the total weight increases slowly, since the fish are still small and cannot consume much food. As they grow bigger, so their capacity to feed and to grow increases, so that the gain in the total weight of the batch of fish accelerates. But, beyond a certain point, the rate of increase begins to slow down. This is because the total weight of the batch of fish, its "biomass", has now increased to the point where there is no longer unlimited food for all, and the individual fish begin to compete with each other. Still the "biomass" increases, but now at a diminishing rate, until finally all further growth stops, for the fish are now making use of all the food available to them without gain or loss in "biomass".

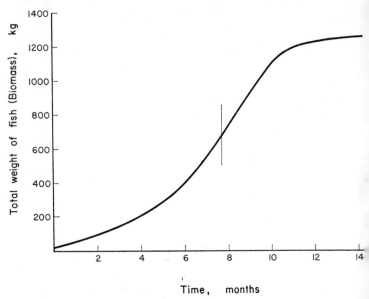

Fig. 5. Graph showing expected increase of biomass of fish population until the maximum standing crop is reached.

This weight of "biomass" is the "maximum standing crop" of that pond under those conditions of management.

For example, in Rhodesia, a series of trials indicated that, for *Tilapia* species, and in that particular fish farm, the maximum standing crops were about:

    800 lb/acre in unfertilized ponds,
  1900 lb/acre in fertilized ponds, and
  5500 lb/acre in fertilized ponds with heavy supplementary
       foddering.

The graph in Fig. 5 shows that it would not be good business to wait until a batch of fish had grown to the maximum standing crop before harvesting and selling. The graph shows that, as the biomass of fish approaches the maximum, its growth slows down, and so its increase in value *with time* slows down. The fish farmer would do much better to harvest the fish crop while it is still growing fast and appreciating in value; then he could restock and take a second crop, and so get a total return from his pond much greater than he would by waiting until the first stocking grows to the maximum.

When fodders are used to supplement the natural production of fish food in a pond, the maximum standing crop of fish which can be supported will depend on how much fodder is given and what is its nutrient value. A very wide range of foodstuffs, mostly waste or by-products of agriculture, such as oil cakes, grains, mill sweepings, etc., may be used, and the food-conversion rates, that is how much fodder is needed to give one part of fish, vary greatly with the nutrient value and digestibility of the fodder. Where the food-conversion rate is high, as when very nutritious fodders such as silkworm pupae are fed in large quantities, the maximum standing crop can be very high indeed. Foddering is a matter of economics, and depends on such things as the price and availability of fodders and fertilizers, the cost of the fingerlings used for stocking, the value of the finished fish according to weight, and the premium, if any, on big fish. The fish farmer has to judge all these things.

When a batch of fish has grown to near the maximum standing crop, so that its rate of growth is slowing down, a partial fishing, or "skimming", may be done. This removal of a part of the fish brings the biomass down again to well below the maximum, and the remaining fish will resume fast growth until once more the maximum standing crop is approached.

On the other hand, when a pond already holds the maximum standing crop of fish, the addition of more fish will cause all the fish to lose weight because there is now not enough food for all;

some of the more emaciated fish will die, and so the biomass is brought back again to the maximum standing crop. This can happen seasonally, for the maximum standing crop will be higher in the summer than in the winter. That is why it is so frequently the practice in temperate climates to harvest the fish in the autumn, selling the marketable fish and redistributing the remainder among the ponds. One of the reasons for the unsatisfactory nature of ready-made but undrainable fishponds such as gravel-pits and open-cast mining pools is that the state of the stock of fish cannot be accurately known, so that both fishing and restocking are a matter of guesswork. There may be too few fish in the pond to use the food available, or there may be so many that little growth is taking place. But in the latter case, the fish will appear to be emaciated, which should tell the fish farmer that there are too many fish, or too little food, or both.

There is an upper limit to the maximum standing crop in a stagnant pond, and that is set by the presence of enough dissolved oxygen to keep the fish actively feeding, and by the accumulation of the harmful waste products of the fish themselves. These factors can be circumvented by growing the fish in cages in running water, veritable battery production, or in small ponds with running water, which assures a plentiful supply of dissolved oxygen, and the sweeping away of the waste products. Trout farms are of this kind; and in Japan and Russia carps may be intensively reared in this way. The rate of fish production can be extremely high, as high as 150 kg/m^2 per annum; but of course in such cases the water simply acts as a support for the fish, and as the means of bringing dissolved oxygen, and removing the waste products. All the fish growth will be due to fodders added in very large quantities.

From what has been said about the maximum standing crop, it would not be possible to do planned work with fish which will breed in the production ponds. This is the great disadvantage of the *Tilapia*, otherwise so very suitable for fish farming. In pond conditions, they begin to breed at a size well below any marketable weight, for example at a length of 9 cm and a weight of 20 g. In a pond where *Tilapia* is breeding, the maximum standing crop will soon be reached, not by the growth, to a marketable size of about 250 g, of the fish originally stocked, but by the breeding of thousands of small, emaciated, and commercially valueless fish.

Because *Tilapia* are otherwise such valuable fish, many trials have been made to prevent or delay this early and too prolific breeding. The most promising method has been to prevent breeding by stocking only one sex, usually the males, because they grow faster than the females. This can be done before breeding begins, and some very good results have been got. Success depends on the exclusion of *every* female fish, for the fish is so prolific that the offspring of a single female could in a few weeks bring about the overcrowding it was desired to avoid. An answer to this, in turn, is to stock some predatory fish with the *Tilapia*, so that if there is any accidental breeding, the fry will be eaten by the predators, and so contribute indirectly to the fish crop.

Another device is to breed *Tilapia* of one sex only, and this was first done at Malacca in 1958, by crossing two species of *Tilapia*. I well remember the growing surprise of my Malay assistant and myself, as we worked over the offspring of these cross-breedings. By the time we had counted 100 males, and not a single female, I realized that we had found something interesting and important. Since then, other cross-breeding among other species of *Tilapia*, in Israel and Africa, has given the same result. Since the hybrid fish cannot breed, because only one sex is present in the pond, and since they grow faster than either parent, these hybrid *Tilapia* are likely to restore *Tilapia* to its rightful place as one of the best of food fishes to farm.

In the Tropics and sub-Tropics, even the common carp may do "wild breeding" in the production ponds, and this has become one of the problems of the very fine Israeli fish farming industry. In Russia, "wild breeding" of the carp is countered by the stocking of rainbow trout, which, in devouring the unwanted young carp, themselves grow to a valuable weight.

In new fishponds, the first stocking must be based on an estimate of the fertility of the soil and water. Fishponds vary as much as individual fields in their natural fertility, and fish farming is not, and never can be, an exact science (nor is any other kind of farming, for that matter).

Making the best estimate he can, the fish farmer will stock his ponds and manage them so as to get what he would consider a reasonable crop. If he gets this crop, he may try to increase his rate of stocking and his rate of fertilization and foddering so as to get a larger crop in the next harvest. If he fails to get the crop he expected, he will stock fewer fish next time. After a few years, he will learn the sort of production he can expect from his farm, and stocking and management will become a routine matter. In any case, fishponds tend to increase in fertility as the years go by.

CHAPTER 11

Fish Farming in the Sea

MANY of the most valuable farm fish have an ability to adapt themselves to living and even flourishing in salty water. Many of the carps will grow in water nearly one-third as salt as the sea, and in fact the common carp can live in the less saline parts of the Baltic Sea. The value of this, from the fish farming aspect, is that water too salty or brackish for most land crops can still be used to grow crops of fish. A recent example of this is near the Dead Sea in Israel. There, trials were done in ponds filled with water having a salinity varying from 2 to 8 parts per mille (the open ocean has an average salinity of 35 parts per mille). The fish cultivated were common carp, hybrids of *Tilapia*, and the grey mullet; and good crops of fish were got. Where fish farming has to compete with agricultural and other interests for a limited water supply, it may be handicapped, especially in the dry season: but a shortage of water need not arise where seawater, or brackish water (dilute seawater) is used for fish farming. As there is an increasing interest in the possibility of fish farming in the sea, a short account will be given here.

For many centuries a kind of fish farming has been carried on in the shallow and sheltered Inland Sea of Japan. This farming includes the cultivation of edible marine seaweeds, of oysters and other shellfish, of prawns and of valuable species of marine fish. The fish may be kept in enclosures in the sea, and fed on small valueless fish to bring them quickly to marketable size.

79

The farming of marine shellfish is world-wide. The newly-settled fry of shellfish, such as oysters, mussels, cockles and clams, may establish themselves in shallow water in far greater numbers than the surroundings will support. So these over-crowded young are transplanted to places where there is a plentiful supply of food and plenty of room to grow. In the oyster pools of Norway, fertilizer may be added to the sea-water, to increase the abundance of the minute algae on which the oysters feed.

Considerable interest has been taken in a trial made, during the last war, in the sea lochs on the west of Scotland. These are sheltered arms of the sea, often deep. Trials were made, to see what effect a given quantity of added fertilizer had on the natural rate of production of these areas.

The addition of a mixture of fertilizers containing potash, phosphorus, and nitrogen had a notable effect. First, the plant plankton showed an enormous increase, and then followed a great increase in the zooplankton, and bottom-living animals. Finally, fish such as the plaice grew up to five times as fast as in unfertilized waters.

These trials were abandoned at the end of the war. This was partly because the rest from fishing had fully restored the stocks of wild sea fish (see page 2), so that the fishing fleets were making very profitable catches. It was also partly because these first trials had shown up some difficulties. For instance, too much of the fertilizer was taken up by the brown seaweeds, which flourished so greatly that there were difficulties with deoxygenation of the water. No species of fish was available to devour, and so use, this extra crop of weed. Finally, the plaice, having grown fast to a large size, migrated out of the lochs and were lost.

Interest in this kind of work is now reviving, partly because overfishing has once more reduced the stocks of wild sea fish, and partly because research has improved the prospects of breeding valuable sea fish such as the plaice and sole, and of providing stocking material to grow in fertilized and enclosed areas of the sea. Large-scale trials are beginning.

Meanwhile, fish farming in brackish water, which is a mixture of seawater and freshwater, has been carried on for centuries in many parts of the world, for example, in India, Indonesia, the Philippines, Hong Kong, Formosa, and all round the Mediterranean Sea. These brackish water fish farms are usually built on land reclaimed from the sea, or on land reclaimed from salt marsh or mangrove swamp. The tidal changes of level are used for the filling and emptying of the ponds, and, where possible, a freshwater stream may be canalized to lead alongside the ponds, so that the seawater can be diluted or flushed out if necessary.

As with freshwater fish farming, the size of the fish crop depends on the management of the ponds. Seawater is always alkaline, and is often rich in nutrient salts; so the ponds may not be fertilized, but may rely for their fish production on algae grown at the expense of nutrient salts brought in with the seawater, and released from the pond mud. In such cases, the rate of fish production may vary, according to the natural fertility of the soil, from as low as 50 kg/ha, which must surely be barely economic, to several hundred kg/ha. With management which includes treatment with rice bran and the taking of several fish crops a year, total production may be as high as 2000 kg/ha.

In Indonesia, the Philippines, and Formosa, the fish grown are principally the milk fish, *Chanos chanos*, a herring-like fish which grows to a very large size, but which is usually marketed at about $\frac{1}{2}$ lb to 1 lb; and the grey mullet (*Mugil* sp., Fig. 4). Both these fish feed on the felt of algae which grows on the pond bottom, and the art of the fish farmer is to encourage the growth of these algae. A rate of production of algae of 25,000 kg/ha will maintain an average production of milk fish of 2000 kg/ha. Only slow-acting fertilizers can be used, for fast-acting fertilizers such as soluble phosphates and nitrates might lead to the growth of plant plankton, which is of little use as food for these fish, while it would kill the algal pasture by shading out the light. So slow-acting organic fertilizers, such as manure or rice bran, are used.

Prawns and crabs usually find their way into the ponds as larvae, with the inflowing seawater, and grow to be a valuable addition to the crop.

Around the Mediterranean, the fish cultivated in the brackish water fish farms are the grey mullets and the eel. I have seen a *valle*, or brackish water fish farm, in the Venetian lagoon, and also a brackish water mullet farm at Arcachon, on the Bay of Biscay. In both cases there is an arrangement to allow freshwater to flow into the farm when available.

In spring, grey mullet and eel fry are collected by allowing a small stream of water to flow out of the sluice gates of the ponds. This current attracts the elvers and young mullet by the thousand; they are caught, counted, and stocked in the fishponds. There they grow all summer and autumn on the natural plant and animal produce of the ponds. In the late autumn, the ponds are fished, the marketable fish are sold off, and the remainder are placed in storage ponds until the spring, when they renew their growth. It is extensive fish farming, with a simple technique, and a low rate of production per hectare. Profit must lie in farming a large area as inexpensively as possible.

Neither the milkfish nor the grey mullet will breed in captivity, but they breed naturally in the open sea. The young are caught on sandy beaches or in estuaries by fishermen, who sell them to the fry dealers. But because of the unreliability of the natural supplies of grey mullet fry, attempts are being made, with promising results, to induce breeding in captivity by stimulating the shedding of the eggs by injections of fish pituitary glands (page 72).

CHAPTER 12

Why Not More Fish Farming?

FISH are more tender than meat, and often sell for as much per lb or kg; and rates of production are higher for fish than for land livestock, especially on poor land. On good permanent grassland in England, young growing cattle can gain 300 lb liveweight per acre of land per annum. On poor tropical pastures, it may be a tenth or less of this. Yet on poor tropical soils, such as those at Malacca, fish production can be made to reach 2500 lb/acre per annum. What then are the obstacles to a rapid extension of fish farming?

1. The idea of fish farming is a novelty outside the countries where it is traditional. All the world over, farmers are a conservative lot, rightly slow to change from ways which have served them well in the past. Moreover, cattle are regarded as walking wealth, conferring prestige on their owner; fishponds as yet are no status symbol.

2. Water must be reliably available the year round, and fish farming is risky where there is a long dry season.

3. There must be security of land tenure, for few would take the trouble, and spend the time and money, to make a fish farm, on land held on an insecure short-term lease.

4. Capital is needed to build the embankments and sluices, and canals to bring water to the ponds, and for the ancillary equipment. But in the so-called underdeveloped countries, where the need for protein foods such as fish is greatest, capital is hard to come by, and such as there is goes to more prestigious schemes.

5. Finally, though fish farming is neither more difficult nor

83

more laborious than other kinds of farming, it fails unless the people have some tradition of intensive livestock husbandry. For example, attempts to propagate fish farming in Latin America have failed for this reason. Fish do need some care and attention, and though they can survive neglect, they will not thrive. In Zambia, for example, ponds seldom receive adequate attention from their owners, who assume that the fish will grow without any attention or management. Nomadic peoples, or peoples practising shifting cultivation, are unlikely recruits for fish farming; though one French author thinks that the establishment of fish ponds, which cannot be carried about, may help nomadic people to settle down.

For all these reasons, fish farming on the peasant scale is best done, in the underdeveloped countries, as part of a mixed smallholding. Again, this is the experience in Zambia, for a man working a smallholding growing vegetables and fruit must visit his garden frequently, and can therefore give some attention to pond management. The ponds would be part of a smallholding including a market garden, fruit trees, pig, duck, and poultry raising, and perhaps silkworm cultivation. The water in the ponds would be a reserve for watering the gardens, and the waste products of the garden and of the livestock would feed the fish either directly or indirectly through the fertilization of the water. Carp grown in ponds to which large flocks of ducks have access may grow two to five times as well as those grown in ponds without ducks; and pig dung may act as a food as well as a fertilizer. Vegetable trash from the garden would feed vegetarian fish. At intervals, the pond bottom would be scraped out and deepened, and the scrapings are an excellent fertilizer for the garden and fruit trees. Such a smallholding would have a variety of produce to sell: fruit, vegetables, pork, poultry, eggs, as well as fish, and would be an economic unit with the fish as probably the best payer. But this system, already in use for ages among Chinese people, might take generation to acquire in many of the underdeveloped countries

Further Reading

HICKLING, C. F. *Fish Culture*. Faber & Faber, London, 1962.

HICKLING, C. F. *Tropical Inland Fisheries*. Longmans, Green, London, 1960.

STEWART, W. D. P. *Nitrogen Fixation in Plants*. University of London, The Athlone Press, 1966.

MACAN, T. T. and WORTHINGTON, E. B. *Life in Lakes and Rivers*. Collins, London, 1951.

MACAN, T. T. *Freshwater Ecology*. Longmans, Green, London, 1963.

RUTTNER, F. *Fundamentals of Limnology*. Translated by D. G. Frey and F. E. J. Fry. University of Toronto Press, 1953.

Index

87